ISBN 978-1-331-43091-9
PIBN 10189225

This book is a reproduction of an important historical work. Forgotten Books uses state-of-the-art technology to digitally reconstruct the work, preserving the original format whilst repairing imperfections present in the aged copy. In rare cases, an imperfection in the original, such as a blemish or missing page, may be replicated in our edition. We do, however, repair the vast majority of imperfections successfully; any imperfections that remain are intentionally left to preserve the state of such historical works.

1 MONTH OF
FREE
READING

at

www.ForgottenBooks.com

By purchasing this book you are
eligible for one month membership to
ForgottenBooks.com, giving you
unlimited access to our entire
collection of over 700,000 titles via
our web site and mobile apps.

To claim your free month visit:
www.forgottenbooks.com/free189225

Similar Books Are Available from
www.forgottenbooks.com

ROGER MILLER;

OR,

Heroism in Humble Life:

A NARRATIVE.

BY GEORGE ORME.

WITH AN INTRODUCTION,

BY JAMES W. ALEXANDER, D.D.

NEW YORK:

ROBERT CARTER & BROTHERS,

No. 285 BROADWAY.

1852.

"'ROGER MILLER' will prove a treasure to every practical philanthropist. I do not remember reading a narrative more admonitory, suggestive, or encouraging. This I can say after thorough examination, for every sentence in the book I have carefully marked. Wherever it goes, a blessing must follow. The usefulness of Mr. Miller in his life was remarkable; it is my impression, that by this faithful record of his trials and labors his influence will be felt for many generations in a degree and to an extent it is impossible to calculate.

"JOHN WADDINGTON.

"9 SURREY SQUARE,
"*April* 9, 1851."

"A more worthy, diligent, kind, and useful person, could not be found in the whole circle of those who are engaged in the service of the poorer classes.—ASHLEY." (*Times.*)

"Their calling is high and holy. Their fame is the property of nations. Their renown will fill the earth in after ages, in proportion as it sounds not far off in their own times."—LORD BROUGHAM.

PREFACE.

THE following pages have been written in the hope that they may be found by many, neither uninteresting nor unprofitable. The life of a good man, abounding in earnest and patient labors for the interests of piety and humanity, and distinguished for usefulness to both, can never be a subject of indifference to rightly constituted minds.

> "Princes and lords are but the breath of kings,
> A *holy* man's the noblest work of God."

But the life of such a man is not only fitted to interest, it is adapted also to become a means of good of the highest order. The influence of a person's character and works does not expire with himself. It may be perpetuated long after he has passed from the field of toil, and become then even more powerful than before.

The Jews, in the days of Christ's earthly sojourn, revered and honored, after death, the memories of those prophets whom before they and their fathers had most bitterly persecuted; and we all know how frequently those who most easily withstood all the commands and counsels of a father, the entreaties and tears of a mother the instructions and exhortations of a teacher or a pastor, while these lived, have after their death felt in their words a power which could be no longer resisted or opposed.

> "The idea of his life has sweetly crept
> Into his study of imagination,
> And every lovely organ of his life

Has come apparelled in more precious habit,
More moving delicate, and full of life,
Into the eye and prospect of his soul,
Than when he lived indeed."

Nor is it those only who were more immediately connected with the individual, and were the objects of his
benevolent solicitudes and labors, that are susceptible
of this influence, but all. To those who, in any department, are engaged in the same great work, his zeal may
afford excitement, his energy impart strength, his modes
of operation give wisdom, and his success yield encouragement; while to those who are dead to God, his whole
history may become a means of conviction and quicken-
ing. And surely we ought not needlessly to allow such
influence to be lost. In a world like ours, where evil is
so much in the ascendant, and has so many and such
mighty agencies enlisted in its favor, we can ill afford to
throw any influence away that is available for the ad-
vancement of truth and righteousness. By all that is
sacred in religion, and dear to humanity, we are bound
to gather it up, to throw it into the great mass that is
sustaining throughout the world the mighty struggle
against evil, and there to diffuse it as widely, and per-
petuate it as long, as may be. These, chiefly, are the
considerations that have influenced the writer in preparing the following Narrative, which now lead him to
send it forth to the world, and which, whatever may
become of it, will be the grounds of his satisfaction in
having done so.

INTRODUCTION.

THE very striking work here reprinted was known to me before the American publishers determined to bring it out. It has already awakened much interest in Great Britain, and is destined to do the like here. For, different as the condition of Europe is from that of America, in many respects, there are some things in which the lessons of one continent are invaluable to the other. And though I am persuaded the exchange in matters of religious enterprise is in our favor on the whole, yet there are some portions of that debatable land, lying between political economy and religion, which have been more thoroughly surveyed and traversed in England than in America. The reason of this is easily found. The evils of old prescriptive abomination, the evils of over-population, pauperism and organized villany, the evils of great cities, in a word, have there become so enormous as to be intolerable. The energetic application of some kind of remedy followed, as a matter of course. We have as much perhaps to learn from British Christians, in regard to territorial subdivision, domiciliary census of vice and woe, schools for the abject, night asylums for the houseless, and courageous plunging into the gulf after perishing felons, as British Christians have to learn of us in regard to wine and whisky, social religious meetings, and church accommodation. In this matter of cities and great towns, their peril was more imminent. The horrible excrescences were fungous and insupportable; no wonder they called for the knife. It will be our wisdom to learn means of preservation from their attempts at cure.

Among a thousand blessings which we enjoy as a free country, for which we ought to bless God every hour of our lives, there are some which belong to us as a new country. Population has not yet trodden on the heels of sustenance. The astounding inequalities of property which in the Old World present to view, on one hand, the plantations and pre-serves of a nobleman who can travel fifty miles on his own land, and on the other hand, roofless, floorless hovels, or parish unions, or crowded jails, barracks, and guard-houses; inequalities sanctified by age, prejudice, and heraldry, do not exist among us. And hence the dishonesty of those clamors by which demagogues turn truth into falsehood, by uttering concerning our own fresh, lovely, agricultural America, sentences which are all too true of England, Scotland, and Ireland. Yet after making every allowance for these diversities, there is a marked tendency towards the ills of the old country. We should be wise in time, and should provide against im-pending evil, by means derived from the experiment of others.

It merits the solemn consideration of every philanthropist, in other words, of every true Christian, that *the cities of America are rapidly becoming like the cities of Europe.* It would be well, indeed, if we imported merely their fash-ions, their luxuries, and their art: we are also rapidly importing their vices. The resemblance is nowhere so striking as in the very lowest strata of society.

The thief or the beggar of New York or New Orleans, is very like the thief or the beggar of Glasgow or Paris. Similar conditions produce the same results. Nay, not only do our cities imitate the vice of the Old World, but they import it ready-made; and even the pickpocket and burglar are often foreign performers, British actors on American boards. The dreadful and indescribable iniquity and wretchedness of the lowest classes in cities, are known by a very small proportion of good people. There is no reason why every philanthropic man should personally inspect these haunts of sordid infamy, any more than that he should enter the small-pox hospital or the insane asylum. Yet are these hundreds of thousands to be left to perdition? Shall we be forever kept at home from going to rescue the publican and the harlot, by beholding some "lion in the way"—some lion of false prudence, some lion of custom, some lion of clerical or ecclesiastical etiquette? One of the great revivals of this stirring, rapid age—

may God grant it speedily—would be a revival of the spirit of the good Samaritan in
all our brethren of the laity. These lines are
not penned to shield or excuse the clergy.
God forbid! Our omissions are innumerable,
and are felt, owned, and repented of daily by
many a servant of Christ. But it is a serious
question, whether individual effort for the
reform of the profligate, and the conversion of
the impenitent, is not less frequent and urgent
than it was even twenty years ago; while our
necessities are greater. We remember with
praise to God such men as Joseph Eastburn,
Harlan Page, Joseph Brewster, and Francis
Markoe, men who went far to seize and restore the single sheep or lamb lost in the
mountains, and we know some such men still
living. We prize and honor, and would aid
in the work of City Missions, and all that
silent but benign labor of the City Tract
Society, in which many excellent men have been
employed for years. But these are the very
persons who best know how few come up to
the help of the Lord by individual effort, by
sacrifice of taste, feeling, and time, by actual

visitation of the wretched, and by personal exhortation of the unconverted. " Money," says a preacher who has ably pleaded this cause, " is given more freely than time, or direct personal effort. If their own tastes are gratified, their own families provided with the means of grace, too many have little regard for others, or for the interests of the church in general."* There are those of us who can remember a much more general activity in seeking out the haters of God, and urging on them the claims of the gospel. Perhaps both erroneous doctrine and imprudent measures sprung up during that revival period, but weeds are apt to be rankest in rich soils. Anything is better than to let sinners go down to ruin, while we sit and muse upon points of orthodoxy, and niceties of prudish decorum. Souls are perishing in our way by myriads. Thousands of professing Christians in our churches are doing nothing

* " Moral Aspect and Destitution of the City of New York. A Discourse at the opening of the Presbytery of New York, Oct. 13, 1851, by the Rev. William Bannard, Pastor of Madison Avenue Presbyterian Church. Charles Scribner, 1851."

in the way of personal exertion to prevent their perdition. From such premises, can there be any conclusion but one?

Let no one hastily raise a cry of fanaticism, as if the summons were to any strange, novel work, or to engage in services unsuited to the individual. The work is the ancient, established, and acknowledged work of religious beneficence, and it is not pretended that every man is fitted for every work. There are some, perhaps, whose bounden duty it is to stay at home. There are some branches of philanthropic duty which would be ill attempted by any but the aged, or by Christian women. Yet there remains a vast field of duty to be performed by Christian men. Too much has been conceded to the mercantile world in this matter, till at length it is not an uncommon thing for Christian professors, and even church-officers, to spend years of life without ever seeing the inside of a cellar or garret, or ever standing by a poor man's dying bed. Such duties they leave, according to the perverted usage of the day, to the gentler sex. So far as this effect of over-hurried business

continues to operate on the church, so far we
may expect God's curse, both on our churches
and our business. The last part of the twenty-
fifth chapter of Matthew still abides in force.

In the following pages, the Ragged Schools
are mentioned. The class for which these
schools are primarily intended does not exist
—let it be said with thanks—in America.
Sporadic cases of abject poverty unquestion-
ably occur, chiefly in the persons of Euro-
peans; but we have not arrived at that stage
in the progress of states, when whole generations of beggary form a sort of recognized
guild.* Yet here a remark made above must
oe repeated; we are treading closely on the
steps of Europe. Already our streets, and
alleys, and suburban fields, and play-grounds
exhibit a close approximation to the class
who fill the Ragged Schools. Methods of the
same general character, modified by differ-

* He who would learn at once how low human nature
may sink amid the vaunted civilization of England, may read
several papers in the "Household Words," the later numbers of Mayhew's "London Labor and London Poor," which
will be reached before long in the American reprint; and the
"Life of a Vagrant," New York, Carter & Bros., 1851.

enees of country and habits, must be speedily employed, or our Sunday news-boys and roller-boys will become a generation of swaggerers and ruffians, ripe for war, piracy, and murder. It has been my privilege to inspect the Ragged Schools of Edinburgh and Glasgow, with a satisfaction which it would be difficult to express. From a number of documents now lying before me, I cannot refrain from extracting some remarks by the eminent clergyman to whom this enterprise owes its origin in Edinburgh, remarks which called forth the public commendation of such men as the late Lord Jeffrey and Lord Murray.

"In a small, well-conditioned town," says Mr. Guthrie, "with the exception of some children basking on the pavement, and playing with the dogs that have gone over with them to enjoy the sunny side, between the hours of ten and one, you miss the Scripture picture of ' boys and girls playing in the street.' Not so in the Grassmarket. On one side of this square, in two thirds of the shops (for we have counted them) spirits are sold. The sheep are near the slaughter-house,—the victims are in the neighborhood of the altars. The mouth of almost every close is filled with loungers, worse than Neapolitan lazzaroni,—

bloated and brutal figures, ragged and wretched old men, bold and fierce-looking women, and many a half-clad mother, shivering in cold winter, her naked feet on the frozen pavement, a skeleton infant in her arms. On a summer day, when in the blessed sunshine and warm air, misery itself will sing: dashing in and out of these closes, careering over the open ground, engaged in their rude games, arrayed in flying drapery, here a leg out and there an arm, are crowds of children: their thin faces tell how ill they are fed; their fearful oaths tell how ill they are reared; and yet the merry laugh, the hearty shout, and screams of delight, as some unfortunate urchin, at leap-frog, measures his length upon the ground, also tell that God made childhood to be happy, and that in the buoyancy of youth even misery will forget itself.

"We will get hold of one of these boys. Poor fellow! it is a bitter day; he has neither shoes nor stockings; his naked feet are red, swollen, cracked, ulcerated with the cold; a thin, thread-worn jacket, with its gaping rents, is all that protects his breast; beneath his shaggy bush of hair he shows a face sharp with want, yet sharp also with intelligence beyond his years. That poor little fellow has learned to be already self-supporting. He has studied the arts;—he is a master of imposture, lying, begging, stealing; and,—small blame to him, but much to those who have neglected him,—he had otherwise pined and perished. So soon as you have satisfied him that you are not connected with the police, you ask him, 'Where is your father?' Now, hear his story,—and there are hundreds could tell a similar tale. 'Where is your father?' 'He is dead, sir.' 'Where is your mother?' 'Dead, too.' 'Where do you stay?' 'Sister and I, and my little brother, live with granny.' 'What is she?' 'She is a widow woman.' 'What does she do?' 'Sells sticks, sir.' 'And can she keep you all?' 'No.' 'Then how do you live?' 'Go about and get bits of meat, sell matches, and sometimes get a trifle from the carriers for running an errand.' 'Do you go to school?' 'No, never was at school; attended sometimes a Sabbath-school, but have not been there for a long time.' 'Do you go to church?' 'Never was in a·church' 'Do you know who made you?' 'Yes, God made me.' 'Do you say your prayers?' 'Yes, mother taught me a prayer before she died; and I say it to granny afore I lie down.' 'Have you a bed?' 'Some straw, sir.'

"Our stranger friend is astonished at this,—not we;—alas! we have ceased to be astonished at any amount of misery suffered, or suffering, in our over-grown cities. 'You have,' says he, 'splendid hospitals, where children are fed, and clothed, and educated, whose parents, in instances not a few, could do all that for them; you have beautiful schools for the gratis education of the children of respectable tradesmen and mechanics: what provision have you made for these children of crime, misery, and misfortune? Let us go and see the remedy which this rich, enlightened Christian city has provided for such a crying evil.' We blush, as we tell him there is none. Let us explain ourselves. Such children cannot pay for education, nor avail themselves of a *gratis* one, even though offered. That little fellow must beg and steal, or he starves: with a number like himself, he goes as regularly to that work of a morning as the merchant to his shop or the tradesman to his place of labor. They are turned out,—driven out sometimes,—to get their meat, like sheep to the hills, or cattle to the field; and if they don't bring home a certain supply, a drunken father and a brutal beating await them.

"For example, I was returning from a meeting one night, about twelve o'clock: it was a fierce blast of wind and rain. In Prince's Street, a piteous voice and a shivering boy pressed me to buy a tract. I asked the child why he was out in such a night, and at such an hour. He had not got his money; he dared not go home without it; he would rather sleep in a stair all night. I thought, as we passed a lamp, that I had seen him before. I asked him if he went to church 'Sometimes to Mr. Guthrie's,' was his reply. On looking again, I now recognized him as one I had occasionally seen in the Cowgate Chapel. Muffled up to meet the weather, he did not recognize me. I asked him what his father was. 'I have no father, sir; he is dead.' His mother? 'She is very poor.' 'But why keep you out here?' and then reluctantly the truth came out. I knew her well, and had visited her wretched dwelling. She was a tall, dark, gaunt, gipsy-looking woman, who, notwithstanding a cap of which it could be but premised that it had once been white, and a gown that it had once been black, had still some traces of one who had seen better days; but, now she was a drunkard, sin had turned her into a monster; and she would have beaten that poor child within an inch of death, if he had been short of the money, by her waste of which she starved him, and fed her own accursed vices. Now, by this anecdote illustrating to my stranger friend the situation of these unhappy children, I added that, nevertheless, they might get education, and secure some measure both of common and Christian knowledge. But mark how, and where. Not as in the days of our blessed Saviour, when the tender mother brought her child for his blessing. The jailer brings them now. Their only passage to school is through the Police-office; their passport is a conviction of crime; and in this Christian and enlightened city it is only within the dark walls of a prison that they are secure either of school or Bible. When one thinks of their own happy boys at home, bounding free on the green, and breathing the fresh air of heaven,—or of the little fellow that climbs a father's knee, and asks the oft-repeated story of Moses or of Joseph,—it is a sad thing to look in through the eyelet of a cell-door, on the weary solitude of a child spelling its way through the Bible. It makes one sick to hear men sing the praises of the fine education of our prisons. How much better and holier were it to tell us of an education that would save the necessity of a prison-school! I like well to see the life-boat, with her brave and devoted crew; but with far more pleasure, from the window of my old country manse, I used to look out on the Bell Rock Tower, standing erect amid the stormy waters, where in the mists of day the bell was rung, and in the darkness of the night the light was kindled; and thereby the mariners were not saved from the wreck, but saved from being wrecked at all. Instead of first punishing crime, and then, through means of a prison education, trying to prevent its repetition, we appeal to men's common sense, common interest, humanity, and Christianity, if it were not better to support a plan which would reverse this process, and seek to prevent, that there may be no occasion to punish.

"But, it may be asked, would not this be accomplished by the existence and multiplication of schools, where, in circumstances of necessity, a gratis education may be obtained? We answer, Certainly not. Look how the thing works, and is working. You open such a school in some poor locality of the city; among the more decent and well-provided children there is a number of shoeless, shirtless, capless, ragged boys, as wild as desert savages. The great mass of those in the district you have not swept into your school ; but grant that through moral influence, or otherwise, you do succeed in bringing out a small per centage,—mark what happens. In a few days this and that one fail to answer at roll-call. Now, an essential element of successful education is regular attendance ; for, in truth, the world would get on as ill were the sun to run his course to-day, and take a rest or play the truant to-morrow, and be so irregular in his movements that no one could count upon his appearance, as will the work of education with an attendance at school constantly broken and interrupted. Feeling this, the teacher seeks the abode of the child, climbs some three or four dark stairs, and finds himself in such an apartment as we have often seen, where there is neither board, bed, nor Bible. Round the cinders, gathered from the street, sit some half-naked children, his poor ragged pupil among the number. 'Your child,' says he to the mother, 'has been away from school.' I pray the Christian public to listen her reply. 'I could not afford to keep him there,' she answers ; 'he *maun* do something for his meat.' I venture to say,—nay, I confidently affirm,—that there are many hundreds of children in these circumstances this day in Edinburgh. I ask the Christian public, What are we to do ? One of two things we must do,—look at them. First, we may leave the boy alone ; by-and-bye he will qualify himself for school. Begging is next neighbor to thieving : he steals, and

is apprehended, cast into prison, and having been
marched along the public street, shackled to a
policeman, and returned to society with the jail-
brand on his brow, any tattered shred of character
that hung loose about him before is now lost. As
the French say, and all the world knows, '*Ce n'est
que le premier pas qui coute.*'   He descends, from
step to step, till a halter closes his unhappy career ;
or he is passed away to a penal settlement, the vic-
tim of a poverty for which he was not to blame, and
of a neglect on the part of others for which a right-
eous God will one day call them to judgment.

" There is another alternative ; and it is that we
advocate.   Remove the obstruction which stands
between that poor child and the schoolmaster and
the Bible,—roll away the stone that lies between
the living and the dead ; and since he cannot
attend your school unless he starves, give him food ;
feed him, in order to educate him ; let it be food of
the plainest, cheapest kind ; but by that food open
his way to school ; by that powerful magnet to a
hungry child, draw him to it.

" Strolling one day with a friend among the ro-
mantic scenery of the Crags and green valleys round
Arthur Seat, we came at length to St. Anthony's
Well, and sat down on the great black stone, to
have a talk with the ragged boys that were pursuing their vocation there.   Their *tinnies* were ready
with a draught of the clear, cold water, in hope of
a halfpenny.   We thought it would be a kindness

to them, and certainly not out of place in us, to tell them of the living water that springeth up to life eternal, and of Him who sat on the stone of Jacob's Well, and who stood in the Temple and cried, 'If any man thirst, let him come unto me and drink.' By way of introduction, we began to question them about schools. As to the boys themselves, one was fatherless,—the son of a poor widow; the father of the other was alive, but a man of low habits and character Both were poorly clothed. The one had never been at school; the other had sometimes attended a Sabbath-school. These two little fellows were self-supporting,—living by such shifts as they were then engaged in. Encouraged by the success of Sheriff Watson, who had the honor to lead this enterprise, the idea of a Destitute School was then floating in my brain; and so, with reference to the scheme, and by way of experiment, I said, 'Would you go to school, if, besides your learning, you were to get breakfast, dinner, and supper there?' It would have done any man's heart good to have seen the flash of joy that broke from the eyes of one of the boys,—the flush of pleasure on his cheek,— as, hearing of three sure meals a-day, he leapt to his feet, and exclaimed, 'Aye will I, sir, and bring the haill *land* too;'* and then, as if afraid I might withdraw what seemed to him so large and munificent an offer, he again exclaimed, 'I'll come for but my dinner, sir.'"

* The whole tenement.

There are undeniable tokens of renewed attention to the wants of our city population. Some churches have long been engaged in a missionary work of this kind, which has come back upon themselves with blessings. Street-preaching, which has been practised for more than a century in Great Britain, is proposed among ourselves. If to this could be added a renewed experiment, under better auspices, towards a supply of FREE CHURCHES, WITH ABLE AND AWAKENING PREACHERS, a visiting of the whole population after Dr. Chalmers's plan,* and a number of day-schools for the most degraded, we could not long remain without the sight of fruit.

The writer of these paragraphs discerns in the subject of the following memoir a Christian brother of another denomination; but this rather adds interest to the narrative. The labors here suggested are those which make men undervalue lesser differences. I trust I speak the mind of thousands in saying

* See Chalmers's Civic and Ecclesiastical Polity of Large Towns.

that I raise both hands and my whole heart to praise God for the work he has wrought among the poor and despised in city and in wilderness by our Methodist brethren. They have often gone where we could not go. Let us follow their example, and share their reward.

It is far from being intended to hold forth Mr. Miller as a model. We neither inculcate his particular opinions—sometimes they are not our own—nor urge his particular methods. But we commend the whole narrative to those city Christians who desire to lessen the alarming mass of human misery, and so serve Christ. Especially do we commend the book to all officers in churches, all Sunday-school teachers, and especially all colporteurs, tract-distributors, and visitors of the poor. The reader who rises from the volume unmoved, and without a glow of new desires to be individually useful to the suffering and the wicked, must be made of sterner stuff than many to whom these pages have been submitted.

ROGER MILLER.

PART I.

ROGER WOODS MILLER was born at Carlisle, September 19, 1808. His father, Ralph Miller, was a Scotchman, and appears to have been gifted with considerable natural talent and great energy of character. He had served in the army as a private soldier for a number of years, but had, a little before this period, while stationed in Scotland, received his discharge. His pension, on retiring from military service, was but ninepence a day; but he was a man of great bodily strength, and of some skill in rock-blasting and canal and road making, and was consequently, able very amply to supplement its deficiencies as an income. He was, however, a man of no prudence, and of no moral principle. Accustemed, as a soldier, to travel about from place to place, he cherished a liking for this kind of life, and seems to have been incapable of settling long in any one locality. Carlisle lay in the course of his wanderings, and on this account, principally, had become the scene of his temporary abode. Though a hus-

band and a father, he appears to have exhibited a
total want of those affections which are proper to
these sacred and endearing names.   Domestic habits
he had none, and, if not " without natural affection,"
he was certainly the slave of vices which prevented
its practical exhibition.   Like too many of the profession in which, for some years, he had lived, and
in part, no doubt, as a consequence of the peculiar
circumstances and influences associated with it, he
was an abandoned and reckless profligate, and expend-
ed upon his own appetites and those of his worthless companions, what ought to have been sacred to
the wants and welfare of his family.   His wife and
children, instead of cherishing with affection and
care, he was accustomed now to abuse with the utmost harshness and cruelty, and then to abandon to
neglect and want.   Some time subsequent to their
settlement at Carlisle be entirely forsook them, and
Mrs. Miller was left with three helpless children to
perish or to subsist as they might.

It was at this time, and under these hard and adverse circumstances, that the subject of the following memoirs was born—a dark and cloudy dawn, not
unsuitable to the short and checkered day by which
it was destined to be succeeded.   A kind and faithful Providence took them under its care, and by
ways and means unknown to us graciously provided
for them.   After the lapse of some time the father
returned, and removed his family into Lancashire;
and here again, after a short period, forsook them.

Mrs. Miller, compelled now to go into the world to seek a livelihood, placed Roger Woods with an elder brother in the workhouse at Blackburn. He was at this time but six years old, but was sent with his brother to work,—first at the print-works of Mr. Turner of that place, and afterwards at those of another gentleman, by whom, at the same time, he was taken into the house. Here, it appears, in addition to the continual confinement, rigid discipline, and the monotonous and wearisome duties of the factory, he was doomed to extreme domestic drudgery, aggravated and embittered by the harshness with which, in a numerous household, he was treated. After a stay of some months in this place, although he had not then completed eight short years of life, his master set himself earnestly to get the boy apprenticed to him until the age of twenty-one. Arrangements for this were actually made, and the hapless child beheld himself ready to be chained for full thirteen tedious years to a family whose severity had rendered them hateful in his eyes, and to a trade that had become an object of the deepest dislike, accompanied by domestic circumstances and treatment extremely degrading and oppressive, and consummated by no very cheering hope of ultimate comfort.

Revolted by the prospect that now opened before him, and exasperated by the sufferings he had already endured, he resolved on effecting his escape. A favorable opportunity soon presented itself, and

without money or clothes save those he wore, and a
small bundle he carried in his hand, this poor forsaken child started for Manchester—a distance of
twenty miles—by a road of which he knew not a
step, hoping there to find his mother, and to mend
his lot.   The journey took him two days and a half
to accomplish.   His own account of the adventure
is touching :—"It was my duty to go each morning
to a distance of two miles for milk.   Taking advantage of this, I got up on the morning of the day appointed (for his apprenticement) earlier than usual.
They supposed it was that I might get back and
be ready sooner to be measured for a new suit of
clothes, and to receive the sum of two shillings for
spending money, which the overseers were to give
on the occasion.   I put my shoes and stockings into
the milk-pan, a shirt in a bundle, and went my way.
After having got about a mile and a half, I put
down the can in a field, and lost no time in getting
into the road for Manchester.   Being very young, I
did not make much progress.   I only got that day
as far as Mr. Turner's print-works ; I there met with
some men and boys whom I knew, and with them
I went in.   The day was then advanced, and one
man told me that if I would be still all night he
would make me a bed with his printing blankets
under one of the tables ; but I must be sure to lay
still, or the watchman would find me out in the
night.   He gave me some food, and I went to rest.
I was woke up several times during the night, but

kept myself still till my hospitable friend came in the morning, who brought me a good breakfast, and food to carry with me on my way. I then commenced afresh my task, which I completed on the following day at noon, having slept the second night in a hay-loft, by the permission of a gentleman to whom it belonged."

On arriving at Manchester, hungry, faint, and foot-sore, clad in tattered garments, and covered with dirt, he set about searching for the object of his fond pursuit, and, by perseverance, succeeded in discovering her. "I was surprised," says the sister, with whom his mother then resided, "one night when doing up the house, where, with my mother, I was then living, at being accosted by my name. I looked and saw a little boy, ragged and dirty, who said, 'Do you not know me, Elizabeth?' It was poor Roger, who had run away, because as he said, they used him cruelly." His mother, who having heard of his flight without knowing its cause, or the direction he had taken, had been almost distracted, now received him as one from the dead, and listened with many tears to the story he rehearsed of the wrongs that had impelled him to flee, and of the hardships he had encountered on his way. "We washed him," says his sister, "cut his hair, and after burning his old clothes, which were all in tatters and so dirty that we put them on the fire with the tongs, we purchased him suitable clothing, and then got him a place at two-and-sixpence a-week."

This "place" was in a cotton factory. "I was then put," says he, referring to this event, "into what is not improperly called 'infant slavery.'" A person who has never visited and carefully investigated a factory of this description, and understands not the way in which such establishments were *then* formed and conducted, would find it impossible adequately to conceive of the unhappiness of a child thus early doomed to labor in them. The atmosphere commonly found in them was extremely close and oppressive, and impregnated throughout with particles of oil and cotton, which gave to it a most offensive and nauseous smell, and rendered it in a great measure unfit for breathing. Their huge, massive, and complicated machinery, presents at best a spectacle truly appalling to the eyes even of adults, especially when unaccustomed to it; while, from its incessant action, there arises a continual, heavy, monotonous noise that drowns every other sound, and perfectly stuns and confounds the ear. A stranger could rarely at that time visit one of these places, and continue in it for the space of but half an hour, without experiencing more or less of headache, and other painful symptoms of physical derangement; and never without being sensible, as he quitted it, of a relief like that he would feel on emerging from a noisome dungeon. Their influence upon the health and spirits of those employed in them was too clearly seen in the blanched cheek, the faded eye, the wasted, decrepid, or distorted form, the unnatural lassitude and debility, and the premature decay, by which they were, for the most part, characterized. The children immured from early morn till eve, within these huge, gloomy, and unwholesome places, were subjected to an oversight the most despotic, vigilant, jealous, and too commonly capricious and cruel. Meanwhile their persons were continually encompassed with danger, and, not unfrequently, by a slight inadvertency, the consequence, in some cases, of weakness and fatigue occasioned by the employment, a garment was caught around a shaft or by a wheel, and in a moment, amid the mighty mass of machinery, the tender form of a child was crushed. It is but fair to add, that these factories are now in general improved in their structure and arrangements, and that, in some instances, no expense or pains are spared to render them as wholesome and pleasant as the case will admit; and the condition and circumstances of those employed in them, especially children, are incomparably better. At that time, however, the system existed in its utmost rigor, and the factories were but little better than prisons.

Such was the character of the places into one of which young Roger was at this early age introduced, and such were the circumstances amidst which he was now cast. Confined here from six in the morning till eight at night, his condition was hard indeed, and was deeply felt to be so by himself. Such was the influence it exerted on his mind that he never, in after life, adverted to the time he spent in the factory without seeming to shudder at the recollection ; or spoke of the system generally acted upon there, without expressing the deepest detestation respecting it, and sympathy for its young and helpless victims.

Some time after his being placed here, his sister married, his mother forsook him, and he was again left to shift for himself. His weekly wages at this time had risen to four shillings. This sum, received at the end of each weary week, he had himself so to lay out as to pay for his lodgings for the past, and provide for the wants of the next.

His education, as might be supposed, had been wholly neglected by his parents ; and, having himself had to give all his time and energies to the work of self-support, he had been unable to repair the consequences of this neglect. And, indeed, engrossed as he was in a continual struggle for mere existence, and exposed, meanwhile, to the influence of circumstances adapted only to debase and deprave, it seems marvellous that he should ever have thought of scholastic or mental improvement at all, or taken a step for its attainment. He had had, however, from an early period, a strong sense of the value of knowledge, and a desire to possess it ; and his way being now opened, he entered with great delight the Sabbath-school connected with the Rev. William Roby's Chapel, Manchester. The instruction offered him in that school is all that, apart from the public ministrations of the Gospel, he ever received ; and who can say to what extent it laid the foundation for, and contributed to, the consummation of his ultimate character and usefulness ?

It is a great and important use of the Sunday-school system, especially as then applied, and as now to a still greater extent applied in the Ragged School, that it rescues the most neglected minds from *absolute ignorance* of letters and of truth, and from *entire hopelessness* of scholastic and other mental acquirements. This is in itself a great advantage, but its value is immensely increased by the influence it is adapted afterwards to exert upon those minds. It never ends with itself, but uniformly and power-fully tends to inspire a taste and awaken aspirations for further improvement, to create confidence as to the practicability of its attainment, and to impart the courage and strength necessary for the purpose. Not unfrequently it has these effects in a very large degree, and so leads to ultimate results of the great-est value.

It was thus in the case of this poor neglected boy. With a mind naturally robust, ardent, active, and enterprising, strengthened and quickened by the adverse circumstances with which at every step he had had to grapple, he had lived to this period with-out having met with any one to introduce him to the first and simplest elements of learning, or to lead him to feel that even these were within his reach. This, however, being now done for him by the Sun day-school, a new and fairer prospect unfolded itself before him,—a fresh and brighter day dawned upon his being,—a new life throbbed in his bosom ; high and unwonted aspirations arose in his spirit ; energies that had slept woke up into activity, and hope scattered a hitherto unknown gladness all around him ; and, animated and strengthened by these, he set himself diligently to labor at the work of self-education. Night after night, on returning to his home, after being shut up within the walls of a gloomy factory for fourteen hours and upwards, enervated with its atmosphere, and worn out by its dull round of duties, he busied himself, without assistance or encouragement from any one, in efforts to learn to write.

In connection with this desire and endeavor after *mental improvement*, the Sunday-school contributed to awaken and call forth the more benevolent sympathies and energies of his nature, and to prepare him for that work in which he afterwards became so distinguished. While receiving the valued instructions of the school, he was led to appropriate a box to the collection of subscriptions for the evangelization of heathen lands, and was wont himself frequently to deposit in it a portion of his own scanty and precious earnings. He also, even at this age, became the subject of intense longings to become himself a missionary of the cross ; and in fact, in the secrecy of his heart, devoted himself to this noble office, and determined to seek the necessary qualifications.

At the age of fourteen, he was bound apprentice to a copperplate printer in Manchester, but his master, it appears, was a worthless man, and in less than three years after, failed in business. Roger was again turned adrift on the sea of life. Incompetent to fill a situation in the trade to which he had been apprenticed, he was some time at a loss what course to take. At length, in his seventeenth year, he opened a barber's shop, and by this means succeeded for some time in supporting himself in comfort and respectability.

In the meantime, he had passed from the benches of the Sunday-school to the chair of a teacher, and had been led to decision on the great subject of personal religion. What were the direct and subordinate causes leading to this important step, and what the circumstances immediately connected with it, do not now appear. The strong probability is, that these causes were the instructions and engagements of the Sunday-school. All, however, that is certainly known is the fact, that in 1825 he was received into the church assembling in Chapel Street, Salford.

It is well known to be the practice of barbers generally, in our large towns, to open their shops and conduct their trade on Lord's-days. This is especially the case with those of an inferior order, and in poorer localities. Such, in fact, is the degraded condition, in a religious point of view, of great masses of the people of our land, that the barber is required to be in attendance during the entire Sabbath, and finds

more employment frequently on that day than in all
the week besides. It is, consequently, the day on
which he principally depends for his support, and to
close his shop on that day is, in a great measure,
to forego this ; the more so, as his customers are apt
to take offence at such a step, and altogether to leave
him. Great, therefore, are the sacrifices, and, for a
time at least, sore the trials of the man, who in this
line of life avows his adherence to Christ, and is concerned for consistency in his deportment and character.

It was so in the case of young Miller. When first
he betook himself to the razor, he appears to have
opened his shop for trade on the Sabbath as on other
days ; but afterwards, on becoming a teacher in the
Sunday-school, and remembering what he had there
himself been taught of the sacredness of the Lord's-
day, he became unhappy, and determined to make
the best use he could of six days of the week, but to
do none but "the Lord's work on the Lord's-day."
This purpose was no sooner formed than acted upon ;
but from that time his business declined. He sustained the trial for some months, but at length, in
1826, things became so unfavorable, that he saw he
must alter his course in some respects or starve. Unhappily, he listened to the advice of some professor
and fellow-member of the same church, less scrupulous than himself, and opened his shop on the Sabbath.
" In a short time after," adds he, impressively and
instructively, " all my real enjoyment in religion, and

all my desire to attend the means of grace, was gone."

To what appalling consequences does one false step give rise! In his case, many dark years of open apostasy and extreme irreligion and vice ensued, and innumerable troubles, both temporal and spiritual, all apparently resulting from this single act. In November, 1826, he married Ann Fielding, of Manchester, whom he had known but three months, and of whom he says, "she made no pretensions to religion;" and in February of the following year, found himself with his wife, through the depressed state of trade, in circumstances of the extremest distress. At her suggestion, he sold off his few goods, and started with her for London, resolved, that if his way should not be opened there, before he was compelled to change his last sovereign, he would "immediately enlist for a soldier."

"I soon found," says he, "that the business of a hairdresser in London was more than I could undertake, and I therefore resolved to try what I could do by getting a master to allow me to finish my apprenticeship as a copperplate printer." In this, through the good providence of God, he was successful, though not until he had reached the point of depression as to his finances, at which, according to his determination, he must have entered the army. The master to whom he had engaged himself, was Mr. Ephraim Brain, of Butcherall Hall, Newgate Street—a good man, a member of the Christian fellowship at Surrey

Chapel, with which he himself afterwards became
united.   'i his gentleman received him into his establishment, and allowed him to complete the period of
his apprenticeship on the most liberal terms.   " I
was permitted to have two thirds of all I earned, according to the prevailing standard of wages."   His
characteristic energy and industry soon rendered him
a proficient in the art.   Partly on this account, and
partly from a generous kindness towards him, his
master gave him a large portion of his best work, and
young Miller often carried away at the end of the
week more wages than many of the journeymen with
whom he wrought.   He was now placed in circumstances of physical comfort, and favored with a degree of temporal prosperity to which he had previously been a stranger.

There are persons to whom the smiles of providen-
tial favor do not seem to occasion spiritual harm,
who, on the contrary, appear to find in these only
additional means and motives for the cultivation and
exercise of piety.   But with the majority it is far
otherwise.   If adversity " has slain its thousands,"
prosperity, " has slain its tens of thousands."   Too
commonly it is but as showers and sunshine to the
roots of vice.   It was so with young Miller.   Feeling that now the amusements and pleasures of the
world were within his reach, he became passionately
enamored of them.   Unhappily, his companions in
labor were men devoted to them.   His naturally
frank, cheerful, and generous disposition was fitted

to make him in himself attractive to any society ;
and his skill and success in his trade, his ample means
of commanding worldly pleasures, and his newly conceived desire for them added to it, rendered him specially so to his dissolute workmates, while his own
naturally social disposition and present particular
state of mind rendered him strongly susceptible of
their influence.   How powerful in such circumstances must that influence have been ! and how perni-
cious its tendency ! He fell beneath it ! Vain amusements and sensual gratifications became the sole objects of his desire, and these he pursued with blind
and delirious eagerness. His home was deserted,
his wife and family abandoned to neglect, and the
fruits of his labor, that should have cheered and
blessed them, were recklessly squandered upon his
own lusts and those of his worthless companions.
One circumstance, it ought to be mentioned, that contributed thus fearfully to corrupt and debase him,
was that of working on Lord's-days,—a practice to
which, in an establishment he entered on quitting
Mr. Brain's, both he and his workmates were systematically allured by a premium which was allowed
them of fifty per cent. upon their ordinary rate of
wages for all they did on these days.

In this condition of debasement and misery he
continued for nine years. Meanwhile, his children
were growing up about him under the worst influences ; their education was wholly neglected, and a
moral atmosphere created and thrown around them

that fostered that waywardness and depravity which afterwards became, both to them and himself, sources of the greatest bitterness. He was not, however, permitted to proceed during all these years in his downward course without frequent and powerful checks of various kinds. "My mind," says he, "was never at rest, but I carried about with me a conscience that was a very hell." And then there were times when .the temporal prosperity, which had but served to stimulate and feed his worst passions, and hurry him from depth to depth of guilt and misery, was remarkably withdrawn, when his sky was again shrouded in clouds, and the tide and the breeze were turned against him.

On finishing the term of his apprenticeship, in conformity with the foolish and mischievous usage of the trade, he treated his fellow-workmen to an expensive supper, which he provided at a public-house. There, amid sounds of revelry and mirth, he continued carousing nearly all night. Meanwhile, his neglected wife, alone in her disconsolate home, had been suddenly seized with an affliction that deprived her of the use of her limbs. On returning to his abode at about four o'clock the next morning, he found her in a condition of the utmost helplessness, in which she continued "for many months." At the same time, trade declined, and employment failed. Without any resources he was cast ashore, and, together with his family, "reduced almost to a state of starvation" At length, to get away from the scenes and associations that had so fearfully accelerated his downward course, he suddenly resolved to return to Manchester. Very quickly his furniture was packed up, and in a few days himself and family were landed in that town. There they found trade depressed, employment unattainable, and were compelled to subsist upon their little stock of household goods. Shortly, this resource failed them, and they were again, with five children, on the brink of want, when, on the call of a former employer, he returned to London—the scene of his greatest temporal prosperity, but of his greatest spiritual prostration. "But," says he, "there was one thing remarkable in connection with this event. I determined, when I got on the coach for London, that I would have nothing to do with my old associates." The course thus happily resolved upon, he was enabled for some weeks rigidly to keep. After this, however, his resolution gradually gave way. He began freely to mingle with his former companions in sin, and so ventured again within the first circlings of that dreadful whirlpool which had before so nearly drawn him into its dark and frightful vortex. At this crisis, he was again rescued by the gracious and wonder-working providence of God.

He had sallied forth one fine Sabbath morning, the last in December, 1837, with a band of his shopmates, one of those aimless, idle, and unhallowed strolls by which working-men in large towns so frequently desecrate God's day, "forsake their own

mercies," and subject themselves to the most demoralizing influences ; and was passing with them the
Chapel in Tottenham Court Road, when a venerable Christian woman, tottering beneath the weight
of years, and slowly wending her way to the house
of God, supported by her staff, placed in each of
their hands a tract.   It was " A Wonder in Three
Worlds."   On returning home he read it, became
impressed and thoughtful, and in the evening of tho
same day attended Craven Chapel   Years had
passed away since he was wont to resort to the
house of God, and now everything appears to have
been fraught with influence and suggestion to his
mind.   The spectacle of so large an assembly of religious worshippers deeply affected him ; the sacred
songs poured forth by the sweet and harmonious
mingling of its many "blest voices uttering joy,"
the solemn devotions in which they united, woke up
thrilling memories of the past, and prompted sad
and sorrowful reflections of the present ; while the
venerable aspect of the minister, as he slowly and
reverently ascended the pulpit, awed his spirit.
The text for the evening was Eph. ii. 1,—" And
you hath he quickened, who were dead in trespasses
and sins."   It was "a message from God unto"
him. . He was deeply affected by the views he
received of his own spiritual debasement and misery,
and of his extreme guilt as aggravated particularly
by the fact of his having formerly made a public
profession of religion.   His own reflections on the

occasion are affecting and instructive. Having
adverted to his fall and subsequent course, he
observes : " How important it is that young persons
especially, who think they stand and make a profession of religion, should 'take heed lest they fall;'
for though it is well to have repentance, and be
humbled thus on account of innumerable sins, yet it
is far better to be without those sins. Oh, that this
had been my case ! Yet, on the contemplation of
the mercy of God towards me, that I am still on
praying ground and pleading terms with Him, I am
overpowered with gratitude.

> " 'Oh, the miracle of grace !
> Tell it round to sinners, tell;
> Men, and fiends, and angels, gaze,
> I am—I am out of hell.' "

During the time in which these important events
were taking place, his wife and children were residing at Manchester. The youngest boy, Walter, had
died there, subsequently to his own leaving. This
event deeply affected him, and led him to think
much of the spiritual condition of the rest of his
family. He wrote to his wife, informing her of his
own change of heart, and directing her to come to
him with their children ; but emphatically stating
his intention to have them sent to a Sunday-school,
and his wish for herself to accompany him to the
house of God. This being fully and joyfully agreed
in, his family were quickly with him. " I then

took," says he, "a small attic, in which we lived at a low rent. As trade was bad, we had sometimes only one meal a-day. But in all this we were more happy than ever we had been before. The children, who had been neglected, now went to day and Sunday schools at Crⁿven, and we ourselves attended the chapel."

In the following April he became a candidate for membership with the church assembling here. His letter on the subject, addressed to the venerable pastor, is interesting. After adverting to the encouragement that had been given him by members of the church to seek this privilege, he says, "I have paused on account of my not being known, and of my dread of falling away; but I feel it to be a solemn duty, and should deem it a privilege of no small value, to sit down at the table of the Lord. I conclude to offer myself as a candidate to your church; and as I have been the servant of sin, so now I pray, that I may be made a servant to the cause of Him whom I have persecuted. Remember me in your prayers, that whether admitted to your church or rejected, I may be a student of the cross, and that my chief grace may be humility."

His union with the church was, from some cause, deferred for several months. In the meantime, he continued regularly and devoutly to attend the public services of God's house, diligently to seek the spiritual welfare of his family, to visit the sick, and to promote meetings for social instruction and prayer.

Under date of September 2, 1838, we have from his own pen the following interesting entry :— " This is the first time I have sat down with the people of God at the Lord's Supper at Craven. Oh ! how solemn is the thought to *me* on taking a retrospective view—*I*, the most undeserving of all, *I* go there as a backslider, as one that has received endless blessings from the hand of God, but never till of late saw my need of a Saviour, although I have professed to know myself, and serve my God. O Lord, forgive the past, and bid me now look forward to 'the prize of my high calling.' Teach me to walk in thy statutes, to love thee more, and serve thee with humility, with reverence, and godly fear. May my communion be with the Father, and his son Jesus Christ ! May this day's proceedings prove to be the beginning of good things to my soul, and its enjoyments but a foretaste of heavenly joys that shall never end ! Lord God, into thy hands I now commit myself. Oh ! teach me thy holy will, and bless me with thy divine presence. Bless my father in Christ and pastor, and his message to us, and grant that as one holy family we may be knit together in love."

PART II.

It is "through much tribulation we must enter the kingdom." That tribulation forms an essential element in the discipline of our heavenly Father, and an indispensable means of fitting us for all the high purposes of our Christian calling; of purifying and elevating our own spiritual nature, fitting it for the reception of divine and celestial wisdom, developing our sympathies with the condition of others, qualifying us for usefulness to them; and finally, of furthering our meetness for " the inheritance of the saints in light." It is accordingly, for the most part, allotted largely to the people of God, particularly such as are destined for special service and reward. It was so with Mr. Miller. He had been admitted again to Christian fellowship but three months, when he was suddenly, and under perhaps the most distressing circumstances, bereaved of his wife, and left alone with the charge of five children, the youngest of them but three days old. She died on Christmas day, 1838.

From the time that he himself had been led to return to God and to find peace and hope through believing, he had exerted himself anxiously and prayerfully to promote the conversion of his wife and family. In the case of the former his efforts appear to have been crowned with success, and now, when called to resign her to death, he was cheered with the hope of a reunion in the skies. The result in the case of his children, the two older particularly, does not appear to have been in any degree so satisfactory. Owing, it may be, to some extent, to the neglect and to the many vitiating influences to which they had previously been exposed, they had become the subjects of a waywardness and perversity which he found himself utterly unable to control. Thomas, the elder, became a source of the most painful affliction and trial. Self-willed, dishonest, and intractable, he forfeited the respect and confidence of all by whom he was employed, and rendered abortive every effort for his welfare. He at length determined to go to sea, and because discountenanced in seeking this object forsook his home for the space of an entire week; his father, meanwhile, with a bleeding heart, pacing the streets of London night and day, almost continually, and led at last to conclude that the wretched boy must have perished in the Thames a miserable suicide. A few months after this he again disappeared. As a last resource his father consented to apprentice him to the sea. The ship to which he was bound was one in the Norway fishery. After a single voyage he ran away, and having travelled full forty miles, arrived at Compstall, near Manchester, destitute and almost naked.

Here he managed, for some time, in various ways, to eke out for himself a poor and precarious subsistence. He was then driven by want to return to his father, and was again sent out to sea. In June, 1844, he was apprenticed on board the Missionary ship "John Williams," and fitted out for his voyage, at great expense to his father. And now the father's heart was filled with joy, fondly hoping the event would be his boy's salvation. "Thanks be to God," exclaimed he, "he is now happy! he has got the desire of his heart. Though he has been at sea for four years, and seen many perils, he has been only among wicked men; but now he is in a ship where every man is pious, and each boy a son of pious parents. May the Lord watch over the interests of the ship, and if permitted to return, may my lad be numbered with them who live by faith on the Son of God!" In this hope, however, he was disappointed, for in December of the same year we find Thomas at Goulbourne, in Australia, 250 miles off Sydney, in the service of Captain Howell, a wealthy magistrate. He afterwards left this place, and at length vanished altogether from the view of his friends, and is supposed to have been lost.

Robert, the next in age, followed in a great degree in his brother's footsteps. From the same causes, he too was apprenticed to the sea, and after a few voyages perished off the coast of Shields.

. But "as was his day, so was his strength." In some notes, written under date of December 25th,

1839, he says, after adverting to these events, and particularly to the death of his wife, of which this was the first anniversary, "Twelve months have since passed away. I acknowledge the hand of God, and own as best what He sees fit to appoint. I can truly say that he has upheld me. He has led me into green pastures, and made me to lie down beside still waters. He has restored my soul, and now shall my head be lifted up. . . . But I must still sit at the feet of Jesus. Humility well becomes such a guilty, worthless worm. Lord, teach me to be humble !"

During all this time, Mr. Miller exhibited uncommon zeal and energy in the cause of the Lord Jesus. The circle of his own family first engaged his efforts, but it did not wholly engross them. Soon after becoming a member of the church at Craven, he established and conducted three prayer-meetings, every week, delivering at each of them a suitable address. He also formed a Bible-class for young men, almost all of whom afterwards became members of the church at Craven, and, as a token of their gratitude and esteem, presented him with a handsome copy of Cruden's "Concordance to the Bible." At the same time he was distinguished for extraordinary activity in visiting the sick and dying.

In the midst of these humble but devoted labors, he frequently looked around on the field of evangelical enterprise occupied by the various great societies of our day, and read with thrilling interest the published reports of their operations.   By these causes, the missionary sympathies and aspirations which he appears first to have conceived in connection with his earliest religious inspirations in the Sabbath-school, were again called forth, and he sighed for a larger sphere and fuller consecration to the great work.   Both of these he at length obtained in connection with " The London City Mission."

This unassuming but great society is one of the most flourishing of those originated by the benevolent, the enterprising, and devoted David Nasmith. It is in every respect one of the most admirable and valuable institutions of the age.   It consists of pious and benevolent individuals of all denominations of evangelical Christians, and its object is to employ intelligent, kind-hearted, godly, and laborious laymen, in the regular and systematic visitation, especially of the poorer classes of London and its vicinity, at their homes, privately to read and expound to them the Scriptures, freely to converse with them on all' religious subjects ; to circulate religious tracts, books, and the Bible ; to hold meetings for prayer and Biblical exposition, and otherwise promote their spiritual, moral, and general instruction and welfare.

No object could be more important, no agency more necessary. London alone contains, at the present time, two millions and a half of people—a number more than twice as great as that of the entire population of Wales ; more than double that of the inhabitants of all other country towns and cities of

England and of the Principality together; and
nearly equal to the whole of that of Scotland. And
this prodigious population is increasing at the rate
of thirty thousand, a number equal to that of the
city of York, every year. Its need of spiritual agency
is not only proportioned to the greatness of its population; it is immensely augmented by their living
upon one spot. Then its relation to all other parts
of these realms, and indeed to mankind at large, is
one of stupendous importance. It is the great em-
porium of the world, and its principal centre of influence. All nations flow into it, and are extensively
and powerfully affected by it, for their weal or woe.
It is in many respects their mighty heart, and upon
it depends largely their moral and general condition.
Everywhere its spirit is diffused, its habits and cus-
toms are reproduced, and its virtues and vices are
reflected. Yet what are its circumstances with reference to the ordinary means of religious instruction
and evangelization? It is well known that they
are such as do not provide for one half of its inhabitants. If every church and chapel in the metropolis were filled by regular hearers, not more than
that number could be accommodated with the ministrations of the Gospel. At present this is very far
from being the case; and yet such are the circumstances of the ministers of religion, as to render private visitation and instruction by many of them all
but impracticable. In reference to the ordinary
means of religious teaching and culture, the condi-

tion of the people of Christian England's great and proud metropolis is worse, by one half, than that of Scotland, Wales, or any other part of our own country, and in fact, in a great degree, than many portions of the heathen world.   It is a startling fact, that Jamaica, Sierra Leone, New Zealand, and some of the Friendly Islands in the South Pacific, are, and have been for years, better provided for than London.

Meanwhile, the most numerous, diversified, and mighty agencies for evil are here concentrated, and at work continually.   Theatres and operas for every class : gin-palaces and beer-shops, accompanied by every conceivable attraction; publications the most lascivious, profane, and infidel, in the utmost variety, sent forth in daily tides over all society ; houses in vast numbers dedicated to debauchery, and an extensive, subtle, and active agency systematically directed to its promotion.

The actual moral and religious condition of a great portion of the people is accordingly, as might be expected, far worse than that of many heathen lands.   Full three fourths of that mighty population live in the habitual neglect of all public worship and sacred teaching.   The Sabbath is very extensively turned into a day of extraordinary traffic, of dissipation, and profane pleasure.   In the eloquent language of a living writer, " In many districts the ordinary market is quickened into the bustle and riot of a fair ; the quiet of the week is broken up by the *carnival* of the Sabbath ; the great volcano of iniquity heaves, and rises, and discharges its desultory contents for miles round . . . and vice holds her saturnalia." There is a vast leaven of infidelity, sometimes more vague, sometimes more decided. There are calculated to be not less than 23,000 habitual drunkards annually found helplessly drunk in the streets; about 150,000 are habitual gin-drinkers. There are, it is stated, 20,000 beggars, 30,000 thieves, 6,000 receivers of stolen goods, 4,000 annually committed for criminal offences, 10,000 persons addicted to gambling, 5,000 houses of ill fame, about 150,000 devoted to debauchery, and 12,000 children being systematically trained to follow in their steps, and fill up their places. Most truly has it been said, " The state of many parts of heathen lands, to which foreign missionaries are sent, is as a paradise compared with many parts of London." " It is a fact," says a discriminating and powerful writer in an early number of the Journal of Civilization (and the case is still substantially the same), "that in St. Giles's and the back streets of Drury Lane, around Westminster Abbey, in the parishes of Bethnal-green and Shoreditch, and nearly all along the Surrey side of the river, a state of social civilization exists as low as is to be found in the far-off regions of Africa. . . . Here in England, in London, perhaps at our own back doors, wretchedness the most acute, infamy the most shocking, exists upon the same square acre with a high condition of luxury and wealth " It is impossible, therefore, to conceive of a more urgent and solemn necessity than that which existed, and which still exists, for some such extraordinary agency as that employed by this body. None such, however, except the Christian Instruction Society, existed previously to this, and that was then very limited in its operations, both as to the time given to them and the sphere they occupied. It was not till after this period, that it began to *set apart* men for its work. " The Pastoral Aid," and " The Scripture Readers' " Societies, have arisen since, and are, in fact, the offspring of the City Mission. When this society commenced its operations in 1835, it had but four agents, now it has 240 ; and most happy, and, in some instances marvellous, are the results that have arisen out of its labors.*

Into the service of the mission Mr. Miller entered in April, 1840. The spirit in which he offered himself for it may be seen from the following observations, written by him at the time :—" I have a long time endeavored to persuade myself that I am not called to this important work ; but, after all, when I read the word of God, and the reports of this and other institutions, I feel compelled to look upon myself as an indolent follower of Christ. I have sought the direction of God, and the advice of many friends, and have taken all pains to be guided aright, and I am now induced, in dependence upon

* See the Reports and Magazines published by the Society.

the all-wise God, to offer myself to the London City
Mission." After passing through the usual exami-
nations he was received, and forthwith appointed to
the district which became the scene of his future
labors. It is that of Broadwall, Lambeth. This
district is bounded on the north by Stamford Street,
on the south by Great Charlotte Street, on the east
by Blackfriars Road, and on the west by various
courts and streets. It contained six streets and
thirteen courts, 449 houses and 719 visitable families, and 1,368 adults. The courts and places are
miserably confined, and without provision for their
being ventilated or cleansed ; they are, consequently,
close and filthy in the extreme. " We have penetrated," says Lord Ashley, referring to this and other
similar localities, " alleys terminating in a cul de sac,
long and narrow like a tobacco-pipe, where air and
sunshine were never known. On one side rose
walls several feet in height, blackened with damp
and slime ; on the other side stood dwellings still
more revolting, while the breadth of the wet and
bestrewed passage would by no means allow us the
full expansion of our arms. We have waited at the
entrance of another of similar character and dimen-
sions, but forbidden by the force and pungency of
the odors to examine its recesses. Pass to another
district, you may think it less confined ; but there
you will see flowing before each hovel, and within
a few feet of it, a broad, black, uncovered stream,
exhaling at every point the most unwholesome

vapors. If there be not a drain, there is a stagnant pool; touch either with your stick, and the mephitic mass will yield up its poisonous gas, like the corrus-cations of soda-water. Here reigns a melancholy silence, seldom broken but by an irritated scold, or a pugnacious drunkard. . . . The interior of the dwellings is in strict keeping, the smaller space of the apartments increasing, of course, the evils that prevail without,—damp, darkness, dirt, and foul air. Many arc wholly destitute of furniture; many contain nothing except a table and a chair; some few have a common bed for *all ages and both sexes;* but a large proportion of the denizens of these regions lie on a heap of rags, more nasty than the floor itself. Happy is the family that can boast of a single room to itself, and in that room a dry corner."

The houses are inhabited chiefly by the lowest order of shoemakers, coal-beavers, dustmen, coster-mongers, small hucksters; and several of the courts particularly, were tenanted wholly by young thieves and prostitutes. The larger and better streets are narrow and badly drained, and are occupied by a population extremely diversified in their social posi-tion and physical circumstances, generally very poor, and, in a religious and moral point of view, most degraded. Of near 700 families, only 88 made any pretensions to attending a place of worship, and 107 were totally destitute of the Scriptures. The Sabbath was neglected, and made a day of business and dissipation. Drunkenness, lewdness, profane swearing, and violence, were almost everywhere predominant, rioting amid the wreck and ruin of all that is dignified or dear in individual, domestic, or social life. The following case, recorded by Mr. Miller, may be regarded as the type of a very numerous class, and may serve to indicate the grand source of their debasement and misery :—" Mr. and Mrs. M——, of —— Place, are great drunkards. Although Mrs. M. has not been able to walk for the last twelve months but by the help of others, she is constantly under the influence of drink. They have a family of five children. The eldest boy has no clothing, save a shirt; the eldest girl has only a ragged frock ; and the rest are so utterly destitute as to be compelled during the cold weather to keep their bed. The room is dark, has no ventilation, and has never been cleaned since they first entered it. There is a single bedstead that serves for one whole family, with a miserable bed, and scanty and filthy covering. The whole scene is one of the extremest wretchedness. On entering on one occasion, I found Mr. M. at dinner. The table had been put close to the bed for the accommodation of his wife, she being destitute of all clothing. They had four pounds of boiled neck of mutton in the lid of a saucepan, which was used as the substitute for a dish. The potatoes were rolling about upon the bare table, and there was not a plate to be seen. The family presented one of the most brutish scenes I ever beheld. I have no hesitation in saying, that

the children have never been properly washed, nor
have had their hair once combed out.   They were
always accustomed to plead poverty ; but on inquiring, I found Mr. M. was in a constant situation, and
had been for many years, and that he was in the
receipt of wages to the amount of £1 5s. per week."
Such was the moral waste he was sent to reclaim
and cultivate.

In the meantime he had married a second wife,
who, as he records, became eminently useful to him,
especially as a helper in his work.   Having removed with his family to the district allotted him, he
devoted himself to its welfare with singular but
characteristic ardor, courage, and perseverance.
The notices left by him of his labors and their results are, with comparatively few exceptions, of the
most general character, and consequently afford very
inadequate means for presenting any but an imper-
fect and meagre sketch of them.   He was a man of
action, not of eloquence ; for the field, not the closet
or the forum.   He had great practical skill and
power, but had not literary tastes and acquirements.
All his sympathies were with the deep, varied, and
wide-spread degradation and misery that lived and
breathed, that wept and groaned, on every hand
around ; and all his aspirations were for its amelioration or removal ; and after this he panted and toil-
ed with an earnestness, patience, and perseverance,
rarely equalled.

His first report was presented in October, 1840,

in which he remarks : " In the course of my visits, I have had much to contend with, as the people seem to be unacquainted with the nature of my work ; but, notwithstanding, I have met with a much more favorable reception than I expected, and am led to believe, that through the goodness of God my labors will be blessed to the locality."

Among the first cases that came before him was one exemplifying strongly, on the one hand, the awful effects of dissipation, and, on the other, the power of early religious training. " At No. 5, —— Place," says he, " I met with a young man, who, when I spoke to him about religion, broke out into the following confession : ' I have lived a most wretched life. My only aim has been to gratify my voluptuous passions. I have spent upon them, during the last twelve years, nearly £14,000. I have never, during the whole of that time, been properly sober. My mother, to whom I have been a perpetual grief, gave me a religious education, and I am persuaded I shall never fail to feel the effects of it on my mind. I am under the accusation of my own conscience continually ; and, sir, eventually it will lead me to repentance not to be repented of, or it will lead me to madness.' "

He was not permitted long to continue his arduous labors without seeing instances of what he felt to be the highest order of usefulness—instances which filled his heart with emotions of joy far more exalted than those of the warrior who sees his arms crowned with victory, and his enemy prostrate at his feet. Calling on September 3, at No. 7, ——— Street, he found in the back kitchen a poor woman extremely ill. "I stated," says he. "what was the object of my visit. She replied, 'The Lord must have sent you to me, for I am most miserable.'" She was under an impression that she had committed "the unpardonable sin," and that there was no hope for her soul. He succeeded in convincing her of her error in this respect, and by persevering attention and teaching was enabled to lead her to what appears to have been a saving acquaintance with the Lord Jesus Christ. "I now see," exclaimed she, "that all my own works are of no use in saving me; that if I am saved, it must be through the righteousness of Christ. But, sir, it is you the Lord has employed to teach me this, and if you had not come to see me I should have died deceiving myself, and hell would have been my eternal doom." "I continued," says Mr. Miller, "to visit her frequently, until Oct. 26th. When calling upon her, she said, 'It will soon be no more with me here, and I am glad of it. The Lord Jesus is my friend, why should I wish to stay away from him?' As I parted from her, she pressed my hand, and said, solemnly and affectionately, 'The Lord be with you, my best of earthly friends, and make you a blessing to the souls of men. Farewell till we meet in heaven!' She paused a few moments, and then said, 'The Lord is my light and my salvation; and a short time after,

'O Jesus ! take me to thyself.'   These were her last words."

His office as a city missionary had to do only with the spiritual welfare of the poor among whom he labored.   But while chiefly seeking this, he also took a lively interest in their temporal circumstances, and often exerted himself greatly in their behalf. " Calling," says he, " in November, 1840, at No. 1, —— Place, I found a poor woman lying in one corner of the room in a state of extreme and dangerous illness.   On inquiring into her condition, she told me as well as she was able, that she had given birth that morning to a still-born child.   A surgeon had been with her, the one provided by the parish, and had prescribed for her, but had left her without medicine, and she had neither money, nor fire, nor food, nor any one to attend her "   In a few minutes Mr. Miller provided her with medical and pecuniary assistance, through which she was restored, and, together with her husband, she became a glad attendant at his religious meeting.

During the following month, he succeeded in inducing a number of females to unite for the distribution of religious tracts among the poor girls " *on the streets*" in and about his district, and by this means was enabled to restore to virtue and respectability a number of these most degraded and wretched creatures.   The following case formed the first fruits :—A member of the little female band above referred to, meeting with one of these debased and

unhappy girls, spoke to her affectionately of her
manner of life, and exhorted and encouraged her to
abandon it.   After some demur and inquiry, the girl
finding that the thing was practicable, and that still
there was hope for her, consented, and was taken to
Mr. Miller's house.   She was a native of Oxford.
Her mother was the keeper of a house of bad repute
in that city.   There, amid the peculiarly debasing
and depraving influences of which such a house is
the centre, she had been born and brought up, and
at length, after being trained for the purpose, had
been by her own mother devoted to infamy.   She
had been sold for £10!   How unnatural! how
monstrous the spirit of that mother! how hard the
lot of that poor girl!   Not harder was the case of
those who were offered in flames as an holocaust to
Moloch, or thrown into the Ganges as a sacrifice to
the fabled God of that river.   She abode at his
house for eight days; after which he obtained for
her admission into the South London Asylum.   Here
he continued to visit and converse with her on subjects pertaining to her spiritual and moral well-
being, and was the means of effecting in her what
appeared to be a gracious and hopeful change.   She
was removed on the 27th of January to Lock's-fields
Asylum ; and, after undergoing four painful operations, was thrown into a wasting condition.   " But,"
says Mr. Miller, " her faith and patience are such as
would render her a pattern to many of greater pretensions.   She rejoices especially in the recollection

that she has been brought to seek the Lord, and expresses the utmost confidence in God, and resignation to his will."

The association of females above referred to was in the following month, through his efforts, united to the " London Female Mission," and became what is now called the " Southwark Auxiliary" to that society. Its constitution and design will appear from a statement published at the time.

" I. This society shall be called ' The Southwark Auxiliary to the London Female Mission.'

" II. The design of the society shall be to promote the moral and spiritual improvement of females.

" III. In order to accomplish this design, the following, amongst other measures, shall be adopted —:

" 1. To form associations of mothers, of unmarried women, and of girls, for the purpose of communicating information calculated to help mothers in training their offspring,—to enlighten the mind, to save from temptation, and direct the energies of young women of good character,—and to assist in training such as are growing up to womanhood, in a manner that may render them a blessing to society.

" 2. To promote the improvement of female servants, and to introduce those of respectable character, when out of place, to the Servant's Home, 3 Millman Place, Bedford Row.

" 3. To secure a temporary refuge, with employment and instruction, for indigent young women of *good* character, through the medium of the Refuge

for Indigent Females, 3ᴀ, Princes Street, Red Lion
Square.

"4. To assist deserving females in finding situations in which they may procure an honest livelihood.

"5. To secure the admission of *fallen* females, de-
sirous of returning to the paths of virtue, into the
Probationary House of the London Female Mission."

And the spirit in which this society arose, and in
which it was subsequently conducted, is well and
affectingly represented in an appeal printed with the
above. It is that of

"THE OUTCAST."

Oh, turn not such a with'ring look
  On one who still can feel ;
Nor, by a cold and harsh rebuke,
  An outcast's misery seal.
But think, ere thus the mourner's sigh,
  The mourner's tears you spurn,
That 'tis perhaps a friend on high
  Who prompts my late return.

Oh, say not, then, the cup of wrath
  I must submit to drain,
When in that safe and narrow path
  I wish to tread again.
It is not thus the Gospel speaks
  To those who cease from sin ;
The soul, Messiah's fold that seeks,
  Is ever welcom'd in.

The haunts of vice might pleasing seem,
  When first I long'd to stray ;
But, oh ! one hour dispelled the dream,
  And dash'd my joys away :

Amidst the crowds in pleasure's bower,
　My heart was still forlorn;
And where I thought to find a flower,
　I only felt a thorn.

And say not that my guilt is great,—
　I know, I feel 'tis true;
But while I groan beneath its weight,
　I hope for pardon too.
Beyond the reach of grace divine
　Myself I have not thrown;
And once at least to guilt like mine
　My Lord has mercy shown.

When such a wandering sheep as I
　Was unto Jesus brought,
And all the cruel standers-by
　A rigid sentence sought:
The feeble reed he would not break,
　Though it was bruised sore;
The gentle words the Saviour spoke
　Were,—" Go, and sin no more."

His home became for a time the office of the Auxiliary; and here all their business, during that period, was transacted. This institution became, in many ways, a most valuable agency to him for usefulness. The following is an instance.

In visiting a family in his district in January, 1841, he met with a young woman who had been taken by a person out of the Magdalen Hospital about a week before, with the promise of a home till he should get her a situation. In this she had been deceived by him. The little money she possessed on leaving the hospital had all been spent, and, she not

knowing what to do, had come here to consult with
a friend.   She said she could not think of going into
service unless with a pious family.   On inquiring into
the case, Mr. Miller found it to be one " of the greatest interest ;" he therefore recommended it to the
Southwark Auxiliary to the Female Mission, who
immediately provided her with what was necessary,
and afterwards found her a situation in the house of
one of the ladies, in which she appears to have conducted herself with perfect propriety.

But there were many still more striking instances of the use he made of this institution, and of the
good he was enabled to accomplish through its agency ; one occurred about this time, which must be
mentioned.   Fanny —— was a native of Tunbridge
Wells.   She had at an early period gone into domestic service, and had occupied a situation in a respectable house in Brighton ; while there, she had
been induced to resort to the theatre, and led to conceive a passion for the stage.   By some means she
became acquainted with the performers, whom she
afterwards accompanied to London.   Soon she found
her way to "the street."   She was a tall and remarkably fine-looking young woman, and was distinguished by great energy of feeling and of purpose.
One vice introduced another, and her entire moral
nature went rapidly to decay : extreme drunkenness
was added to other forms of the grossest licentious-
ness, and in all she became singularly bold, shame-

less, abandoned. There was no description of wicked-ness from which she would shrink.

Not unfrequently would she steal away at early day with the clothes of the wretched men whom she had caught by " her much fair speech and flat-tering words," and pawned them for drink before they arose from their miserable couch of sin and shame. The watchman of Farringdon Street she fearlessly defied, and more than once felled to the ground. She was, in fact, the terror of the neigh-borhood, and even the police, from very fear, ab-stained from interference with her, and carefully stood aloof. She continued in this downward course, until at length, in a fit of drunkenness and despera-tion, amid the darkness and silence of night, when the mighty mass of London's population were assem-bled in scenes of pleasure or gathered around their peaceful hearths, this wretched slave of sin had hurried, with dismal and tumultuous thoughts, to Waterloo Bridge, and was in the act of casting her-self from its fearful height into the Thames below, when a stranger, passing, arrested and saved her. She was taken to a neighboring house, and subse-quently to Mr. Miller. She was then but twenty-two. . There were no signs of remorse or shame for her past manner of life, and no solicitude to be res-cued from it. She abode with Mr. Miller near a fortnight, and then entered the White Lion Street Female Penitentiary; for her admission into which, in the meantime, he had provided. Here she continned for somewhat more than six months, at an expense of five shillings per week, obtained by him for her; after which, for her good conduct, she was transferred to the Meard Street Asylum, and provided for freely. She was a good needlewoman, and as such became useful in the institution. She was also a person of general practical ability, and of active disposition; she, accordingly, conceived a wish to leave the asylum for service; and, being opposed in this, effected her escape from the institution. Mr. Miller, on hearing of it, hastened in pursuit of her. He found her in a private house, and induced her to accompany him to the house of a lady of the Committee of Management; in connection with whom he succeeded in getting her furnished with suitable personal clothing, and introduced her to a situation in a respectable family as a domestic servant. She continued in service for upwards of two years. She was then married by a respectable artisan in London, a widower with two children. Both he and his children, who before were poor and wretched, notwithstanding constant employment, became under her management comfortable in their circumstances, and respectable in their appearance; and their home, that had been distracted and joyless, became the scene of order and happiness. She also, with her husband, commenced occasional attendance on public worship, which they had been accustomed wholly to neglect; and frequently, in after years, did she weep most bitterly

at the remembrance of her guilt and shame. She
continued in frequent and intimate intercourse with
Mr. Miller and his family, and often said that she
looked upon him as her father, and that she could
not have loved him more had he been such. They
both fell victims to the terrible pestilence that
swept the Metropolis and devastated so many homes
and hearts in the summer of 1849. After having
assiduously watched and tenderly soothed one of his
daughters, who fell beneath that scourge, they both
retired to die by it themselves,—the daughter expired on the Thursday, and they on the following
Sunday.

Many of these poor creatures, amidst all the levity
they exhibit, he found were the subjects of deep-felt
dissatisfaction with the way in which they were living,
and secret longings to escape from it. The following
case, which occurred to him in his visits during
March in the same year, will exemplify this :—At No.
5, —— Court, he found a young woman, who said
she should be glad if she could get out of such a
course of sin, but feared this was impossible. She
said, " I am well convinced of its wickedness, and
when I think of it, it is more than I can bear. The
thought often drives me to drinking ; and what will
be the end of it I cannot tell."

One of the effects of his labors was the prevalence
of an esteem and love for the word of God, where
that word had been neglected and despised. On
visiting, in the May of this year, one court, he says,

—"Mrs. ——, of No. 5, called to me and said, 'I want to see you before you leave the court.' I accordingly called upon her, and found her full of joy. 'I've got a Bible, sir,' exclaimed she; 'and *so* cheap.' Then, going to her cupboard, she brought forth her treasure, and holding it up for me to view, said,—'There, sir, how much do you think I gave for that?' I observed, 'It is without backs; I suppose you have given fourpence a pound for it.' 'Yes, I have; and it cost me ninepence at the butter shop. Is it not a shame that the word of God should be served so?' Then, after a short pause, she added,—'But I must not be too hard upon the poor creatures, as I should have done the same myself before you came to see me.'"

As might be supposed, his work was frequently attended with great difficulties, and required no ordinary measure of courage. Nor was that courage at any time wanting to him. The following case will illustrate this. "In —— Court there were three men who were the terror of the place. Having repeatedly heard of their determined violence against me, and of their saying that they would kick me out of their house if I should go there when they were at home—a threat which all the neighbors believed they would accomplish—I at once resolved to call upon them; and as they were only at home on Sundays, I arranged to visit their families on one of these days. I accordingly did so. The neighbors, on seeing me enter the first house, were alarmed, and held themselves in readiness to interfere, in the event of violence. The family was at breakfast ; I apologized. The man bid me make no apologies, as he had heard of me, and knew that my intention was good. I had a long talk with him, and the result was that he assured me that he should be glad to see me at any time, and he thought he should begin to go to some place of worship." The effect was much the same in the other two cases.

There was one court (and there were several of the kind) notorious for its extreme, gross, desperate depravity. It was almost wholly made up of bad houses. Their wretched inmates had so uniformly and rudely insulted all religious visitors that called upon them, that these had all at length given them up. "I determined," says Mr. Miller, "to see the keepers of the houses severally, and if possible to reason with them, in order to get access for ourselves and our tracts." He accordingly did so, and this plan had, in a great measure, the effect desired. In connection with tracts, he also gave them his card, as his custom was in all such cases, and assured them of his readiness, at any time, to assist such as might wish to leave their vicious way of living. This step greatly contributed to obtain for him their esteem and kind regard. After this, Christian visitors found no difficulty in getting access to them, and one of these, an aged man, who had been engaged as a tract distributor for twenty years in the neighborhood, and now renewed his peaceful and beneficent labors, meeting Mr. Miller some time after, said to him, " Why, friend Miller, what have you been doing in —— Court ' Formerly, the people would not have my tracts, and would tell me that if I came there, they would put me on the fire, but now they tell me they are *obliged* to me.   May the blessing of God still attend your labors, my dear friend !''

As an instance of his diversified modes of operation, and the spirit with which he engaged in them, the following case may be recorded—" As I sat at dinner on the 15th of June, 1841, a man came before the front of the house with a lot of machinery to amuse the people with, a coach-wheel, a ladder, and a number of pipes.   He first, with great labor, balanced the pipes on his chin, and then engaged to balance the ladder, with a boy standing on the top of it, but first required the crowd to give him some money.   There were about 300 persons present, so, while he was collecting, I determined to distribute tracts, and took with me a quantity of ' The Brazen Serpent.'   As soon as I began to move, the ring was broken up.   The people rushed to me for the tracts, many of them thanking me for them.   One man tore his into pieces, on which I expostulated and reasoned with him.   He at length went off amid the groans of the people, and made all haste to get round the corner of the street.''

" On returning home, on Thursday the 17th, I found a poor young woman, who had obtained from a gentleman one of my cards, and had come to my house to request me either to get her into an asylum, or to effect, if possible, her restoration to her home. It being too late to take her home that night, I paid for her night's lodging, and early on the following day set off, with her directions, to seek her parents. I found all in accordance with what she had said. They are very comfortably situated, her father hav- ing an income of £100 per annum. When they heard of their child, they were deeply affected, and immediately consented to receive her to their home. I accordingly returned, and taking her with me back again, restored her to the arms of her mother. Their meeting together was a touching sight. I took my leave of the now happy mother and daughter, hav- ing first commended them to God in prayer."

The condition of the children, with whom the streets and courts of his district were swarmed, was extremely deplorable. In general, they were aban- doued to the utmost neglect, were ragged and filthy in their persons and attire ; they were also as untu- tored in mind as the most degraded Indian or Hot- tentot brood. They were left to run wild upon the streets, and at an almost incredibly early age, had learned to utter language the most obscene and pro- fane. Neglected in his own childhood, and still deeply feeling the sad consequences of this, he knew well how to commiserate the case of the poor ; and for him to commiserate any case was to set about seeking its relief. His was not so much a sentimen-

tal as a practical compassion. From the first, he
looked upon the condition of these children with the
deepest concern—a concern amounting almost to distress—and set himself about devising for it a remedy.
His plan was, in the first place, to set on foot an infant school. This, for some months, he found himself unable to accomplish ; but by that determined
and persevering industry which was one of his greatest characteristics, he succeeded at length in enlist-
ing for his project the sympathies of benevolent individuals ; and so, before he had completed his first
year of labor, he beheld it carried into effect. Eighty
children were at once received into the school, of
whom seventy-three had never before been within
any such place. These, in the course of a few
months, increased to 160, of whom 128 were here,
for the first time, brought under school teaching and
discipline.

Referring to this institution some time afterwards,
he says—"It is of great value to me in my visits to
the people, as by it their prejudices are subdued, and
kindliness is excited towards me. It is also an
asylum indeed to many of the poor children themselves. Their parents bring them at eighteen
months old, and not unfrequently before they are
weaned ; and it is now no unusual thing to hear
children at play on the district singing some of their
school hymns, or pieces, who, but for it, would, in
all probability, have been singing profane and lascivious songs instead." A pleasing incident connected

with it, recorded by him, may be here inserted. Two of the children, named John and Mary ——, fell victims to scarlet fever ; calling upon their mourning mother shortly after, he received the following statement :—" As they lay together in their last afflotion, John began to sing—

 "'I think when I read that sweet story of old,
 When Jesus was here among men ;
 How he called little children as lambs to his fold,
 I should like to have been with them then.
 I wish that his hand had been placed on my head,
 That his arms had been thrown around me ;
 And that I might have seen his kind look when he said—'

here he stopped, being interrupted by his sister, who after repeatedly trying to join him, but finding herself unable, through weakness, gave it up, and wished her brother to do so too. ' But,' says he, ' sister, I must sing,' and so proceeded with the words—

 "' Let the little ones come unto me.' "

In less than an hour after they both slept in death.

The school became in his hands an important agency for good, indirectly, also to the parents and friends of the children. Here is an example : "Mr. and Mrs. B——, of —— Place, were extremely poor and ignorant, and were in their persons, house, and children, uncommonly filthy. When I first called upon them, and told them the business and purpose of my visit, Mr. B., vociferating a stunning oath, bid me begone, and never again trouble him ' with

any of that 'ere nonsense.' I left a tract, and said,
'I will call again at some future day.' 'Yes, you
do,' replied he, ' and I will soon kick you out—that's
all.' I however called. He was not at home himself, but I met with his wife, and found her but little better than him. Her children, I saw, were in
her way, and occasioned her much vexation ; so I
invited her to send them to the infant school, repre-
senting to her the advantage that would arise out
of this, as she would herself get rid of them during
the day, and they would learn to read. I offered,
if she would wash their hands and faces, to take
them with me immediately. I accordingly did take
them. This care for her children pleased her much.
I continued to visit them, and after some months
again met with Mr. B. at home. In the meantime,
his children had received considerable instruction,
and amongst other things, had learned to sing a number of pretty little hymns, and he himself had been
called to task but a few days before, for commen-
cing dinner without saying grace ; so instead of ' kick-
ing out' his friend, as he had *threatened*, he received him most respectfully. 'I don't know how
it is,' said he, ' but the children seem to learn a great
deal at your school ; I should like to come and see
them.' The man, who, however," says Mr. Miller,
"was more of a bear than a man in temper, was
quite subdued and won. He began to attend a place
of worship himself, became increasingly regular in

doing so, and ended 'an anxious inquirer for the best things.' "

In visiting the people for whom he lived and labored, he frequently met with cases of sorrow and distress, that required great discretion and wisdom, as well as warm and tender sympathy; and afforded occasion for the most beneficial exercise of both. Nor was he wanting in these valuable attributes when they were demanded. Calling, in November, 1842, at a house in —— Place, he found a neat and clean-looking woman, who had recently taken up her abode there. She appeared dejected, and seemed anxious to avoid him. She took a tract with which he presented her, and was about to close the door, but by a little artifice he succeeded in preventing this, when he proceeded to state the object of his visit, and to engage her attention to his message of love. "I soon found," says Mr. Miller, "that she was the subject of grief; and that it was on this account she tried to shun me." He therefore sought the more earnestly to obtain an interview with her, and gradually advanced within, as she retired and became evidently more open to conversation. "After a short time, I was requested," says he, "to take a seat, while she began to tell me her tale of trouble. Her husband, she said, had formerly been a professor of religion, but now never entered a place of worship; that he had altogether ceased to care for her, and had given his heart to another woman, whom he kept; that not less than four times he had broken up her home, and driven her to seek with her parents a shelter; and that still he constantly abused her in the bitterest manner. 'As to my poor soul,' she affectingly added, 'I know that it is in a most dangerous state. Into a church, or chapel, I never go, or if I do and it is found out, I am beaten in the most shameful manner What can I do? shall I stay here to be treated worse than a dog? I shall be glad if you can advise me.' I said, 'If I should advise you to leave your husband, this would be most agreeable to your feelings; but this, a Christian, I cannot do. My advice is, that you stand your ground, and look to the Lord for direction and support. Tell him all your sorrows, and seek his favor and his help, through Jesus Christ, and he will uphold and guide you. At the same time, act in a kind and cautious manner towards your husband. Forget all that is past, try to keep your house, and all that is in it, in the greatest order, especially when he is at home; but see that you make the Lord your trust." He then read a portion of the sacred word, and knelt with her in prayer. "She wept much;" thanked him affectionately for his advice, and hoped, as she said, "the Lord would enable her to follow it."

At No. 17, —— Court, there resided an aged woman who, when he commenced calling upon her, offered a very determined and offensive sort of resistance to him in his work. "She refused my tracts," says he, "and told me she would have 'none of my religious nonsense.' Seeing a little girl sitting near, evidently her grand-daughter, I gave the child a little book containing pictures, which pleased her not a little, and left." He continued to call from time to time, till at length the poor woman began to converse more freely and kindly with him, and took his tracts ; not, however, for herself, but, as she said, " for the child." In April, 1841, he commenced a prayer-meeting near her house, and invited her, in common with others, to attend. She refused to do so, on the ground that her husband would not allow her to go to such places. But one night she heard the singing, and as her husband was not at home, she was induced to steal away there. " At the close," says he, " I gave her my hand, and invited her to come again. ' You have no need to ask me,' said she, ' for neither husband, nor anybody else, shall stop me from coming. It is the first time for thirty years, and I have been thinking what a fool I have been all this time. I'll come again, sir, let what will come of it.' She afterwards mentioned it herself to her husband, when he said, ' If I know you to go there again, you and I shall have a fight.' ' Nay,' said she, ' we won't do anything of the kind —there needs two in a fight. You may abuse me, but you will not get me to fight ; and *after* you have abused me I will go, for I have been an old fool long enough.' ' Well,' said he, ' I tell you once for all, if you go to any such place, I will break your legs, and then you cannot go.' ' I do not think,' she replied, ' you would be monster enough for that ; but

if you should, then the missionary would come to
see me—so break on, but go I will.   If I neglect my
home, you will have cause to complain, but not till
then.' "   Some time after, she wanted to buy herself
a dress, but her husband said she should not have
one at his expense, for if she would " go to a gospel-
house," she should go " in rags ;" he would not
" pay for anything to go there in."   She was often
tempted to stay away, because, as she thought, people
looked at her in her mean attire : but then again,
as she said, " the thought came, if I stop away the
devil and my old man will have just what they want,
and so I said I'll go, for the Lord only looks at the
heart."   She accordingly continued regularly to attend Mr. Miller's meeting, to go to public worship
on the Sabbath, and to endure in silence all her
troubles.   Eventually one of her relations called
upon her, and after some remarks about her going
to chapel, said, " I have bought you a gown, friend,
and if you will get it made up you are welcome to it."
" As soon as she saw me," says Mr. Miller, " at my
next visit, she said, ' Here is the devil cheated again,'
and proceeded to relate the above story."   She continued a regular attendant at the house of God, and
gave pleasing evidence of a hopeful acquaintance
with the truth.

During the month of August, 1841, a lady called
upon him, and informed him of a young woman, the
daughter of a Christian minister in the country, who
was an inmate of a noted house of bad fame in the

neighborhood, who lay ill there, and was supposed to be near death. He immediately determined to seek her rescue, and hastened to the house where she resided. It was one of the worst. He therefore took with him a friend,—a precaution he not unfrequently adopted. They found her in a miserable kitchen with three other girls at her bed-side. " I said to her, ' Is your name —— ?' She replied, ' It is.' I told her who I was ; assured her that though a stranger to her, I would be her friend, if she would allow me ; and said, ' Will you go into an hospital if I introduce you ?' ' Yes,' she replied, ' I will go anywhere with you, if you can get me out of this place.' I forthwith called a cab, and had her conveyed to Guy's Hospital, where she was immediately admitted, and in two hours from the time of my going to her, she was comfortably lodged in the hospital."

She continued here for some time. He then got her into an asylum. At both he regularly and frequently visited her, furnished her with tracts, and otherwise sought to promote her moral and religious restoration. From the first her heart was opened to attend to the things she had read and heard ; and it became increasingly evident that a thorough change of character was being wrought in her. In the meantime she became anxious to return to her friends. Her father was the minister of a respectable Baptist congregation in a provincial town, and two of her brothers were prosperous tradesmen : one at the west end of London, the other in Birmingham.

He wrote to all of them. They treated his letters
with all respect, but "would have nothing to do
with her." Her father determinedly resisted it, and
would not yield to anything that Mr. Miller could
say. For eighteen months he labored for her restoration to her friends without being able to effect it.
At length the girl's health becoming worse, through
excessive confinement, her father consented, on the
assurance of Mr. Miller's confidence in her, to take
her home again ; and also engaged (for he was a
widower), in case of her continuing steady, to commit
the entire charge of his house to her. She accordingly
returned. The expenses of her journey were defray-
ed for her. She was received by her father with
great affection, and soon gave him the most decisive
and affecting evidence not only that she had truly
returned to the paths of filial duty and of virtue, but
also, that "she was most anxious to be restored to
her heavenly Father, from whom she felt she had
wandered still more awfully." She became a candidate for union with the people of God, and her
father had the intense delight of welcoming her into
the fold and flock placed beneath his own pastoral
care. She subsequently became very active and
useful in the cause of Christ, particularly in connection with Sunday-schools, one of which she commenced ; and as to the girl's department, superin-
tended. She at length returned to London, and
entered into business, was married by a tradesman,
and has continued to this day, in every point of view,

a highly respectable member of society. Language cannot express the views and feelings with which she ever afterwards regarded her benefactor.

There were a vast number of cases in which, though, in the notices left of them, they present nothing of a *striking* character, his labors were a means of the highest good. The following may be mentioned as the type of a numerous class. Mr. and Mrs. ——, of 25, —— Street, were a somewhat aged couple. They had long lived together, strangers to themselves and to God; rarely if ever attending a place of worship, and entertaining the most perfect contempt for religion. "At first when I called," says Mr. Miller, "they would not hear anything I had to say, but I continued my visits. They gradually became more and more free and friendly, and at length I was permitted to read and pray with them." After this, his calls were always received with smiles of welcome and of pleasure. Their minds were opened to receive his instructions and counsels, and they became hopefully converted to God. Writing of them early in April, 1841, he says, "The case of this poor man and his wife, at my last visit, appeared truly affecting. Both wept like children, and said with great feeling, 'Oh, sir, if you had not come to us as you did, we should still have been living in our sins. And we have often wondered that you should have troubled yourself to come a second time to see us, as we used you so bad when you first called on us. We never go to bed now or get up without praying for you, as we know that others serve you as we did, when you came to us at first.' 'But, oh! what mercy,' exclaimed the old man, ' has the Lord bestowed on us, to think that he should send his Son to die for a poor old sinner such as I am.' " The poor old man was soon after visited with an attack of paralysis which occasioned his confinement to his room. His wife became a member of the Wesleyan Society in Broadwall.

During the first year of his labors, 28 persons most of whom had been flagrantly immoral and irreligious, were reclaimed; 65 induced regularly to attend public worship; 5 were introduced to Christian churches; and 13 more in health, and 4 in affliction and death, were brought to what appeared a saving knowledge of the truth; 29 copies of the sacred word were distributed, and upwards of 16,000 tracts put into circulation.

"But what are these among so many?" Such, both as to the persons benefited, and the means of usefulness employed for the rest, was the language of his burdened and yearning spirit. He felt oppressively and painfully the comparative littleness of these results, and especially the vast disproportion between his own capabilities and the agencies he wielded, on the one hand; and on the other the magnitude of the evil everywhere surrounding him, and the stupendous greatness of the work required to be accomplished. He accordingly set himself, amid the multiplicity of his own labors, during the first year of his settlement in Broadwall, to form, in connection with Surrey Chapel, an auxiliary to the City Mission; and notwithstanding some unfavorable prejudice and more indifference in the minds of many, he, in conjunction with his excellent superinten- dent, J. H. Harris, Esq., succeeded in so far preparing the way, that at a public meeting held in the chapel at the close of the year, it was organized and estab- lished. A ladies' branch was subsequently added, and first a second, and then a third missionary were called in. It still continues in vigorous and effective operation, scattering the richest blessings of heaven among the most abject and impoverished children of earth.

It was eminently his endeavor to "sow beside all waters," and it was not unfrequently his happiness to find fruit where it might least have been expect- ed. On Saturday, February 5, 1842, the late Mr. Ducrow was to be interred, and an announcement having appeared in the papers that his entire stud of horses were to follow him, it was expected that vast numbers of people would assemble to witness it, which turned out to be the case. Before eight o'clock the whole of the York and Westminster Roads were crowded with spectators. Anticipating this, he obtained grants of tracts from various per- sons to the number of 4,000, and thus equipped, went forth into the immense concourse of people to scatter his seed. "I distributed," says he, "3,000, and was surprised and delighted with the eager manner in which they were received. On the evening of the same day, a friend of mine was met by a young man who had been to see the sight, and who told him that he had seen a gentleman there giving away tracts. "I got one," added he, "and I hope I shall never forget the thoughts it gave rise to in my mind, while reading it." It was headed, "Prepare to meet thy God."

His compassionate concern for poor dishonored females, the readiness with which he embraced their cases when they sought for moral and social restoration, and the ability and success with which he labored for this, became extensively known amongst the benevolent and pious, and occasioned great numbers of these unhappy creatures to be sent to him. Early in the present year a Christian tract distributor, engaged in his noiseless labors of love, met with one of these poor girls just turned fourteen years of age, who, weary of her way of life, was anxious to get out of it. She was brought to Mr. Miller. It turned out she was the child of infamy, and had herself been systematically trained in it by her abandoned mother, who died but a few days after her unhappy girl was brought to him. He first obtained her admission to an asylum, and afterwards, at her own earnest desire, to the Lock Hospital. On being discharged, she was destitute of home and friends, and knew not whither to betake herself. She dreaded to be thrown back into her former shame and misery. She returned to Mr. Miller. For a few moments he hesitated over the case, not knowing what, in the first place, to do with her; " and, as I hesitated," says he, " she, with evident concern and alarm, exclaimed, ' Oh! Mr. Miller, do not let me be turned into the streets again. I will do anything sooner than this.' She belonged to the parish of Lambeth, and to the guardians'of this parish, with her consent, I accordingly took her. They immediately received her into the house, and thanked me heartily for my attention to her." The poor girl would not afterwards go out alone lest she should meet with any of her former companions.

His was a department of Christian labor in which especially he felt that " he that observeth the wind shall not sow, and he that regardeth the clouds shall not reap;" and in which it was indispensable to act in the spirit of the Divine direction, " In the morning sow thy seed, and in the evening withhold not thy hand, for thou knowest not which shall prosper, this or that." Himself an instance of the usefulness of such a mode of Christian labor, he was never at a loss for a motive and an encouragement to engage in it. And he not unfrequently found the seed he sowed with the most solicitude and doubt was the first to spring up, to repay his labor and refresh his wearied spirit. " As," says he, " I was first brought to think of going to a place of worship myself by having a tract put into my hand on a

Sunday morning after a stroll, I feel a delight in giving them." He was accordingly accustomed on a Sabbath morning frequently to go forth to those parts in the neighborhood of his district which were most thronged with idlers, and there to scatter his tracts as copiously as he could. "I put one," says he, "into the hand of a young man who happened to be passing. It was headed, 'Ye must be born again.' The young man followed me for a time, and then asked me if I would allow him to call at my house. I replied in the affirmative, and gave him my card. On the day following he called upon me and told me a long and painful story about his sister, who had bartered away her honor and abandoned herself to infamy." Mr. Miller took the opportunity of speaking to the young man himself on the things that belonged to his peace. The young man said that his father was a widower; that his mother had been a great drunkard; that she had often, to get drink, pawned his clothes, and prevented him from going out on the Sunday; and that as he looked upon her when she lay in her coffin he smiled upon her corpse, and thanked God (for her death). He himself had also been a poor slave to intemperance and dissipation. Mr. Miller found that the tract he had given him the day before had been read, and had made a deep impression on his mind. He presented him with others. He then sought out the unhappy sister, and obtained for her admission to the hospitable inclosure of an asylum, where she afterwards conducted herself virtuously, and was restored to credit and society. Meanwhile, he continued, both personally and through various tracts and books, to seek the spiritual recovery of her brother; nor did he seek this without success. The young man became a regular attendant on the public services of Surrey Chapel. Mr. Miller then sought to induce his father to attend; and soon father and son were seen neatly and respectably attired resorting to the house of God. The latter subsequently became a teacher in one of the numerous Sabbath-schools connected with that chapel, and was at length received into fellowship with the church. "He is now," says Mr. Miller, speaking of him some months after, " an affectionate brother, and a dutiful son, though with great sacrifice to himself. He is also wishful to be a faithful soldier of the Lord Jesus Christ." His sister also exhibited encouraging evidence of a gracious change of heart.

Every opportunity of getting into contact with the most debased and depraved portions of our metropolitan population was seized by him with promptitude and eagerness, and improved with the utmost diligence and care. Having learned that Good, the murderer, was to be executed on the 23d of May, 1842, and anticipating a great concourse of the worst characters, he furnished himself with a large number of suitable tracts, and at an early hour of the awful day was on the spot at work with them. " I was at the front of the Old Bailey soon after four o'clock in the morning. To my surprise, there were even then from three to four thousand people assembled. My motive for being there so soon was, to supply those with tracts who would get close to the gallows, and especially to see the class of persons who got there so early, The morning being fine, was very favorable to my purpose. I counted no less than ninety prostitutes, who, with the men that were with them, were strewed about in a way the most shocking—some sitting and some lying upon the pavement. Many of the men were drunk, and used the most abusive language to me when they were presented with tracts; but those who were sober, received my tracts with all kindness and good feeling The crowd constantly increased, and by six o'clock became immense. I kept continually near the outside, and when the unhappy man was brought out upon the scaffold, found myself in Ludgate Hill. I was not a little pleased to find that numbers of people were not only eager to get the tracts, but also to read them. I distributed 5,500. I saw, however, that it would have been impossible to have done any such thing had it been left to the last."

Resistance to him in his work, far from preventing his going forward, was wont only to arouse him to more determined and careful effort, which not unfrequently resulted in partial or perfect triumph. Distributing tracts in the street one Sabbath morning near the end of the same month, he placed one in the hand of a little man who, he knew, had made a profession of religion, but had grievously fallen. The wretched man threw back the tract, and used abusive language. He was a widower, and had one child, a girl, who attended Surrey Chapel. This girl was with him at the time. Mr. Miller took this treatment with submission and silence. He, however, embraced the earliest opportunity of calling upon him at his home. He was now enraged, "cursed both me and the tract," says Mr. Miller, "threw it back furiously into my face, and bid me leave his house. I said, 'My friend, it would be very unwise for me to leave you in such a rage without first inquiring for the cause. Pray, is it the tract that you are offended at, or is it myself? I do not think, though you have cursed me, that you really would wish either me or any fellow-sinner to be cursed, would you?' 'Why, no,' said he, 'that is not right, certainly; but you know I have been deceived by a lot of professors of religion, and I now go to no place of worship.' 'Well, but,' said I, 'God has not deceived you, has he?' 'No,' said he, 'he has not.' 'But,' said I again, 'have you not acted deceitfully with him? What would be your condition if you were to die now?' 'Why,' said he, 'it would be a bad one, sir; I am wicked, and I am miserable.' 'So you may well be,' said I; 'you have not prayed for some months past, I know. Can you expect to be happy? You have "left off to be wise," and now you are not content to go to hell yourself alone, but you are taking your child there with you,—that child which is the only relic of your beloved wife, now numbered with the dead. Is this as it ought to be? How can you so trifle with the soul of that child by keeping her from the Sabbath-school?' 'Oh! spare me, sir,' he exclaimed; 'I know you are right, and I am wrong, and all you have said is very true. It is not God that has been unfaithful, but it is me. I ought to have gone to God in my troubles, and not to have done as I have; but I thank you, sir, and I hope it will be a warning to me. I hope you will come again soon.'" He began again to attend public worship at Surrey Chapel.

To persons of the most revolting and seemingly hopeless character, he addressed himself without despairing of success, and rarely did he find himself to have altogether labored in vain. There resided at No. 12 —— Place, a man whose personal appearance and character were truly appalling. His frame was uncommonly tall and athletic; his face was singularly large, and environed with huge gray whiskers; his eyes were big, fiery, and restless; and his entire countenance the index of a dark, perturbed, and savage soul. He had seen his threescore years and ten, a greater part of which he had spent at sea. His manners were eminently of that rough and boisterous character that distinguishes a genuine tar, and which seem like the moral reflection and counterpart of the ocean on which he lives. He had also acquired all that coarse vulgarity, profaneness, sensnality, and violence, that too often characterize the sons of the ocean. Their manners and habits he still retained, and they were now accompanied by great surliness and irritability of temper, the result of age and adversity. Undaunted and undoubting, notwithstanding, Mr. Miller called upon him, presented him with tracts, and sought to engage his attention to religious instruction. For nearly eighteen months his tracts were rejected, and he was abused. He, however, still proceeded. Calling at his house on the 18th October, 1842, Mr. Miller found him from home, but met with his wife, who said to him, " I hope, sir, you will not neglect to call and speak to my husband, though he is such a blackguard, and has so insulted you before." " You may depend upon it," said Mr. Miller, " I do not mean to neglect him." " At this moment he came in. As he entered the door, he beheld me, and immediately stood still, as if to stop up the way. He looked at me very angrily; and surveyed me from head to foot. I saluted him in the kindest manner I could, and said, ' I am glad to see you better than when I last called.' He looked first at his wife, and then again at me, and said ill-naturedly, ' Well, and if I am better, is it anything to you? I have not to thank you for it.' ' No, my friend, but I hope you will not neglect to thank God for it ; he is our great friend, and let me tell you that he has promised to do far more than this for you, if you will seek him.'

'Well, but what do you want here?' said he, sav-
agely; and shaking a big stick in my face, he
added, 'I told you before not to come here any more,
did not I?' 'I have come,' I said, 'to read to you
the word of God, and to pray for you that God may
change your heart before you die, for if you die in
your present state you can have no hope of heaven.'
'Will this tract put a loaf of bread on my table?'
demanded he. 'It may,' said I, 'do more than that,
if you read it with a prayerful heart; for I tell you
confidently, that if you will seek heaven in preference
to this world's pleasures, God will bless you.' At
this moment, the wife took up the subject, and said,
'You have always been very cross with this gentleman, and you know he comes from the chapel where
they visited you from' (referring to Surrey Chapel,
and some visitation and relief he had had, while ill,
from its noble benevolent society); 'you certainly
ought to be civil to them.' This seemed to subdue
him, and he put down his stick. I then said, 'But
I hope you will not be friendly with me merely on
that account, for that will be of no good, nor do I
desire your kind feeling on this account; I did not
even know that you had been visited by any person
beside myself.' He then said, 'Well, I have no time
now, but if you will leave the tract I will read it.
As to praying, I must think about that, and you can
call again.'" It is pleasing to add, that in twelve
months after this, as the result of Mr. Miller's persevering labor, this aged sinner had become a regu-

lar attendant on public worship, expressed deep interest in the services of the sanctuary, and earnest hope that he should continue to attend them as long as he might live.

During the present year a special effort was made for the spiritual good of that important and valuable body of men—the Metropolitan Police. To him, in connection with one or two other of his brethren, the work was entrusted; and a letter subsequently addressed to him by a pious sergeant, may serve to indicate at once the manner in which it was done and received, and the influence which it originated :—

"January 30, 1843.

"DEAR SIR: At length I have a little leisure, and gladly avail myself of it, for the purpose of addressing you on the subject of your little book, issued to the whole of the Metropolitan Police force. And I have first, as a member of that force, to thank you for the Christian, benevolent intentions, thus manifested towards the whole. . . It has indeed a long time been a source of the deepest sorrow to my mind, to witness the almost entire disregard to eternal things amongst that portion of the men forming my own district; and the occasional opportunities I have had of mingling with others with whom I am not so immediately connected, give sad demonstration to the fact, that a fearful majority of the entire number are not merely living without God and without hope in the world, but dishonoring and blaspheming the name of the Most High, and indulging in habits alike degrading to the character, injurious to the body, and destructive to the soul. There are, it is true, many exceptions to these grosser immoralities to which I have alluded : in some, perhaps, from more refined intellect, in others from superior education, or parental instruction and example; but where these exceptions may be made, there is still the absence of all desire for the things that belong to their eternal peace. There are also some further (happy) exceptions; but alas! they are few, very few,—so few, that when I meet with one, I am reminded of the poet's lines:

> ' Broad is the road that leads to death,
>   And thousands walk together there;
> While wisdom shows a narrow path,
>   With here and there a traveller.'

"But, sir, I am happy to bear testimony to the fact, that your little tract, so far as my observation extended, was received with a respect and attention which at once surprised and gratified me; and I do think, for the most part, it had at least an attentive perusal. And I find also that many have carefully preserved them; and who can tell but another, or another, or another perusal may be accompanied by the Divine blessing? and who, also, can tell but that these little books may, in some instances, be beforehand, and prove an antidote to the baneful effects of others now abroad, calculated to lead or confirm them in errors destructive to their immortal spirits? And, oh! what an acquisition to the force, and what valuable servants to the public, would some of these men be, had they the fear of God before their eyes. But, alas, it is proverbial among them, and I except no rank, that a policeman cannot be religious; and some indeed say, he don't ought to be, or have a very scrupulous conscience; that he has no time to attend to God's house, or to read God's word, whereas many such will sacrifice much of the precious Sabbath, enough to scan every page of a Sunday newspaper, and those publications so disgraceful to their patrons, so injurious to their readers.

"But I have wandered from the information required of me, namely, if any good results have come under my notice. Now, if my answer was this—none, I would reiterate my for-

mer remarks, to urge and beseech you to a patient continu-
ance in well-doing, seeing such necessity exists as I have
shown. But, sir, I have reason to hope, that the reading of
your society's letter did, at least for the time, in many produce consideration ; and as consideration, you know, precedes
conviction, as conviction does conversion, you will not in this
matter despise small things, but hope that the seed thus
sown shall be as bread cast upon the waters, found after
many days. One man belonging to us, of no mean capacity,
in whom I had never witnessed any concern about his soul,
spoke to me on the subject of your letter, and spoke kindly
too of the individuals by whom they had been presented.
Finding he had read it with attention and apparent satisfaction, I recommended to his notice another book, Mr. James'
'Anxious Inquirer,' and from conversations I have since had
with him, as well as his subsequent attendance on the
means of grace, I may at least say of him, 'He is not far
from the kingdom of God.' May God carry on and perfect
in him his good work ! .   .   .   .

    " I am, dear sir, yours most respectfully,

                    " ——— ———.''

There was one place in Mr. Miller's district distinguished strongly by its extreme filthiness, and by
the gross and almost unmixed depravity of its inhabitants. "It is," says Mr. Miller, "never cleaned
by any of the authorities, and some of the houses
seem never to have had the floors washed from the
time they were first built. The filth and stench are
almost unbearable." The place contained an average of about twenty families, chiefly of the lowest
Irish, almost continually shifting. They are nearly
all thieves and prostitutes—all, that is, from about
twelve years old and upwards. It is a sink of in-

famy : rarely would decency permit him to enter
their rooms. He was commonly compelled to remain
outside to escape the loathsome and revolting spee-
tacles within, while he addressed to them some
words of instruction, of warning, and of exhortation.
Where he could, he scattered his tracts, and distributed his card as a guide to any one who might desire to leave their criminal and wretched way of
living, and as a pledge to each of his assistance.
Nor did he ever despair. " In fact," says he, " I
have more hope of these than of many others, especially those who are always inventing tales to awak-
en sympathy and obtain temporal relief." Nor was
he altogether disappointed in the hope he cherished
with respect to them. There was a poor girl just
twenty years of age, and who but four months before had been a respectable servant, who had heard
him at various times speaking to her landlady, and
was now filled with a sense of the sinfulness of her
way, and came to the determination to starve rather
than continue any longer to live by it or in it. She
soon found herself in danger of doing so ; she neither
had money, nor means of honorably getting it ; had
neither parents nor friends to whom she could fly for
shelter or relief. She continued to abide in the
house, but was steady to her purpose of abandoning
her way of life. Her landlady discovering it, harsh-
ly said to her, " Don't you intend to go out and get
some money ?—you owe me already for three nights."
The girl brst into tears, and said, " I cannot go out."

"If that be it," said the landlady, "you had better go to that parson-man that comes here with tracts, and he will tell you how to get into the society." "She inquired," says Mr. Miller, "for my address, and immediately came off to my house. She repeated her call several times before she found me at home, thus showing the earnestness of her desire and purpose. She told me her painful story. I felt fully convinced the girl was sincere, and promised to do all I could for her." He supported her from his own table for several days, during which he sought to open the way for her introduction into a penitentiary, in which at length he obtained for her an asylnm.

Being known extensively as the devoted and affectionate friend of these poor creatures, he was frequently resorted to for counsel and aid, not only by themselves, but also by their friends; and all seemed to feel the fullest confidence, that if they could but get their cases before him they were sure of assistance and of success.

Mary —— was the only child of a very respectable tradesman, and had been "cherished like a garden flower." Her fond mother had brought her up indulgently, gratifying her wishes, but overlooking her faults and protecting her in them. She was the more indulgent because of the extreme severity of the father. As might be expected, she became wayward, disobedient, headstrong, towards her mother, and set her at defiance. In opposition to her parent's injunctions, she accustomed herself to remain out at night till a late hour, always, however, taking care to get home before her father. At length, when about sixteen years of age, she was led to resort to a neighboring fair, where she stayed till it was too late to return home without incurring her father's displeasure. She was induced to remain out the whole night. The poor girl fell into the hands of an artful seducer, and was ruined. The afflicted mother hastened to lay the case before Mr. Miller, and to seek his aid. At her request he set on foot means of tracing the girl to her place of concealment, which after a few days he succeeded in discovering. The unhappy father, however, on learning the facts, refused to receive her again into his house. 'I have kept on my business for her,' exclaimed he bitterly, 'more than for anything else ; but now my character is so stained by my only child, I will sell all off and leave London.' He accordingly did quit the metropolis, having sold his business for £500. He, however, proposed to give a considerable donation to any asylum which would receive her, and into one of these excellent institutions she was at length, through the efforts of Mr. Miller, and the agency of the Southwark Auxiliary to the London Female Mission, safely lodged. She ultimately married with comfort and respectability.

By many of these wretched outcasts he was, after their restoration by his instrumentality, blessed as their greatest benefactor. Walking one day along the street, a respectable-looking and well-dressed female accosted him. "Mr. Miller," said she modestly, "I hope you will pardon me for speaking to you in the streets, but I was going to your house to thank you for your kindness to me. I am now able to get a respectable and comfortable living. I have been in service for twelve months and all through your kindness." " I was surprised," says Mr. Miller, " for I had lost all knowledge of her, and I said to her, ' How have I been of service to you ? What is your name ?' When she told me I was very much delighted. It was a young woman I had got into a probationary house two years and a half before. She was at the time in a good situation in a highly respectable family in the Blackfriars Road."

During the year 1843 his mind became much affected with the extreme illiteracy and mental degradation of many of the adult females of his district. " Many," says he, " who are mothers, are unable to write or read " For some time this perplexed him, but at length he was led to open for them an adult school. This he first intrusted to the care of several ladies who promised to take charge of it ; but afterwards he committed it to his wife and a few young ladies whom the late excellent Mrs. Sherman sent to aid her. The attendance quickly increased from thirteen to thirty-four. They met together every Thursday evening ; and in connection with devotional exercises, conducted by himself, were taught reading, writing, and arithmetic, and, by an occasional short lecture, were instructed in Divine truth and human duty.

In connection with a statistical account of his district taken about this time (Feb. 1843), he writes, "It will be seen in —— Court, where there were near *fifty families*, there are now but *five women* of ill-fame. Three years since every house was a brothel, and all the court a den of thieves."

In a brief and hasty review of his labors, and their results, at the close of his third year's engagement in the service of the London City Mission, he states—" Besides the formation of the adult and the infant schools, that of the Southwark Auxiliaries to the City Mission and the London Female Mission, the establishment of a Circulating Library, containing 70 volumes, eighteen fallen girls have been restored, fifteen of whom are doing well, and one of whom has gone into eternity, leaving pleasing evidence of repentance towards God and faith in the Lord Jesus, and thirty-four persons have been hopefully converted to God."

PART III.

"Cast thy bread upon the waters and it shall be found after many days," is a divine utterance which, considered by him as referring especially to such labors as his own, ever guided and animated him in them. And many pleasing cases occurred to verify to him its assurance, and to crown his hope. Here is one :—

"Calling one day, in September 1844, at 34, —— Street, I met," says he, "with Mrs. M——, a woman whom I had visited some two years and a half before in Guy's Hospital. She left the hospital as 'incurable,' and as I had not seen or heard of her afterwards, I had concluded she was dead. Her illness had made so great a change in her appearance, that I had no recollection of her person. But as I entered her house she instantly knew me, and addressed me by my name. I was not a little surprised to find out who she was, and felt anxious to know whether she had profited by the instructions I had given her so long before. I asked her if she still remembered these. 'Yes,' said she, 'and I shall never forget them as long as I live. I cannot now neglect the house of God as I used to do, for the Lord has, I trust, made me to feel the blessedness of that new birth of which you spoke to me. The world has nothing in it now that I could love so much as Christ. All is indeed vanity and vexation of spirit.' Interrupting her, I said, 'And what about your husband; is he still unconverted?' 'Yes, sir, he is so,' said she, 'and that is my chief trouble now. I would do anything to get him to go to the house of God. But as God had patience with me, so must I have with him, and I must and I will pray for him. And I hope, sir, you will pray for him too.'"

Another pleasing instance of usefulness in relation to a very important case, occurred in connection with his labors about this time. A gentleman walking one Sabbath evening in a principal thoroughfare, met with a young person whose case deeply affected his mind. Her personal appearance was interesting; she was of middle size, slender form, fair complexion, remarkably beautiful features, genteel attire, and modest bearing. Her appearance and manners altogether were those of a highly cultivated and virtuous lady. Reserve, dignity, and delicacy were all blended in her air, and an atmosphere of purity seemed to encircle her which appeared to forbid every suspicion of her virtue, but which served only to render more melancholy the fact of its loss; there was still, apparently, a lingering sense of its excellence, although the priceless jewel itself had been cast away. She was a poor devotee of shame, weary, however, of her course, and convinced of its wickedness; she was wishful to be rescued, but knew not where to look for it. Her age was then but nineteen years, and, what is astounding, she was all the time supported by a respectable medical man, to whom she was engaged. Information of the case was sent to the Rev. James Sherman, and forwarded by that gentleman to Mr. Miller. Immediately Mr. Miller hastened to the house in which she resided. He found her from home, but left his card, with a message of his intention to call in the evening. From doubtful motives, for she knew not what was his object, she awaited his arrival, and was standing at the door when he got there. She occupied the front parlor of the house, for which, and its furniture, she paid the enormous rent of 25s. per week. She was extremely unhappy in mind about her degraded and criminal way of life, and expressed earnest desire to be taken out of it. "I gave her," says he, " my card, and told her to call upon me at a time I mentioned, promising to do my best to further her wishes. She came, and a long conversation ensued between her, Mrs. Miller, and myself." He found that she had friends at the west end of London who were highly respectable, and deemed it most desirable to effect, if possible, her restoration to them. Having obtained her approval of this plan, he set himself about carrying it into effect; nor did he labor in vain. After a few days she was restored to her brother, who was a respectable tradesman, and who affectionately embraced her and received her to his house. She became an assiduous, tender, and devoted attendant on his afflicted wife, and ultimately settled as the wife of the medical man to whom she had been before engaged.

Near the same time a case engaged his attention, which, though painful to contemplate, may serve to some extent to illustrate what is at length happily occupying very largely the public mind,—the dark mysteries of London life "Late in the night of the last Sunday in October, 1843, when going up stairs on my way to bed, I heard the cry of a child and the shriek of a woman proceeding from some place behind my house. I threw up the window, and found that it came from an adjoining yard. I hastened to the spot, and learned from an almost frantic female, to whom it belonged, that a young woman had been discovered in the yard not only trying to conceal the birth of a child, but also as it was supposed, to destroy its life. Having sent my wife to attend the wretched woman, I went for Mr. Shea, a neighboring surgeon, who in a few minutes was in attendance, and spared no pains for the safety of the child and its wicked mother. She was one of those miserable votaries of shame who at that time swarmed in the neighborhood of Waterloo Road; she was without shoes, and her bare feet was seen protruding through her stockings. She was then but eighteen years of age. Being asked what she intended to do for a living for herself and child, she said, ' I shall do what I have done before ; and as the child is living, he must do as others do if he still lives.' 'What is that?' I asked. 'Why,' she said, 'there is plenty of children get a good living by stealing, and so shall he.'" She was subsequently removed to Lambeth Union House. So filthy was she, that the poor women in the house refused to touch her.

Early in the present year (1844), a new and interesting sphere for holy and benevolent enterprise was opened to him, which he immediately entered; it was in the casual ward of St. Saviour's Union House. It is a well-known fact that there is always a large mass of people in London utterly destitute of home. Until a few years ago, these people were left without any adequate legal provision for their accommodation. And as they beheld the night falling around them, and the blithe and gladsome throngs of the great metropolis skimming gaily along its brilliant thoroughfares to their cheerful abodes, saw themselves without a shelter whither to retreat, or a place in that wilderness of life where to rest their weary limbs. Vast numbers would betake themselves to the public parks, and, seated with their backs against the trees, would seek beneath the chilling shade of these to relieve their weary, worn-out forms, to waste the dismal hours of night, and, if they might, to obtain, at least in some degree and form, the favor of

"'Tired nature's sweet restorer, balmy sleep."

Others betook themselves to the streets, especially

in winter, and beneath the frosty shadow of the
workhouse, or some more friendly wall, or strewed
upon the cold, hard pavement stones, would seek
some sorry shelter and repose, grouping thickly
together and pressing closely upon each other, to
mitigate if they could the rigors of the night by the
mutual warmth of their emaciated bodies, and
hoping that their forlorn and wretched condition
might move to compassion the parish or the police
authorities, and obtain for them relief at least in
some degree and shape.   The condition of these
miserable creatures, however, had, for some time
before this, become a prominent subject of public
attention, and of some general sympathy.   In many
of the workhouses wards had been opened to receive
them for the night, a provision made for their immediate wants, and a breakfast supplied for them
before their departure on the following morning.
Such was the case at the workhouse of St. Saviour's
Union ; and Mr. Miller, perceiving the value of the
opportunity thus afforded for usefulness, threw himself, with all the Christian sympathy and influence
he could carry with him, into the midst of the wan
and woe-begone throngs that crowded eagerly together within this asylum.   Writing of them at
the end of April, he says, "Finding that their
spiritual condition was not thought of in the great
arrangement, I resolved to visit them every night
from seven to eight o'clock, which I have done for
the last three weeks.   Their numbers are from ten

to fifty a-night, and are always made up of new-comers ; so that the total number of them with whom I come in contact is very great.   Many of the poor creatures when they come in, are in the filthiest condition, some in a high state of fever, and sometimes a group of them is sent together to the fever hospital, without delay.   Among them I have found very many who have been members of Christian churches, particularly of the Wesleyan body, but who had wandered from the truth, and many who have been in Sabbath-schools.   Those I feel to claim my special attention."   His method was to read to them the sacred Scriptures, to converse with them in a spirit of kindness and familiarity, especially on subjects relating to their moral and spiritual well-being, to give interesting tracts and hand-bills to such as could read, and to offer prayer with them on behalf of all.   " My visits," says he, " are very favorably received by these poor creatures, and great attention is paid by them while I read the Scriptures and engage in prayer.   I know not that I may ever see any fruit from these endeavors, yet I cannot be unmindful of the Scripture which says, ' Blessed are ye which sow beside all waters.' "

The following remarks of his respecting these curious and painfully interesting gatherings, and the influence of this new and kindly provision made for them, may not be regarded as unworthy of notice :—" It is a pleasing thing to see so many of these wretched creatures each night protected from the inclement weather, who but for this would be exposed to it; but the intended good has also evils mixed up with it. The report has gone forth throughout the towns and villages of the country, that if the poor come to London they will be able to get a night's lodging, with supper and breakfast (freely); and this, coupled with the notion that there are many advantages to be met with here, that according to the old adage 'its streets are paved with gold,' has led many to come to town who would not have done so, and thus has served to swell the numbers of these poor wanderers. I here state only what I have gleaned in conversation with many of them."

Welcome in general were his visits of mercy to the sons and daughters of affliction, and not unfrequently were his seasonable counsels and teaching to them a means of good of the best description. Here is an instance. Mr. F——, of ——, was a shrewd Irish Protestant, and a staunch teetotaller. He ordinarily attended Surrey Chapel, and had received clear and impressive views of spiritual truth and evangelical doctrines under its able minister. He was visited with successive and extreme afflictions for about three years continually, first in the person of his wife, who, after a long affliction, was taken from him; then in a child, of whom he was also bereaved; and finally, in his own person. During all this time Mr. Miller was his constant and faithful Christian visitor and teacher. The poor man was led to see the hand of God in his affliction, and that that hand was one of the purest mercy, that smote him only to humble, that afterwards it might exalt him. He was led to feel himself a great sinner, and with deep humiliation to seek mercy of God in Christ. "I trust," said he to his friend, "it is not presumption in me to believe that he (the Lord Jesus) is able and willing to save even such a sinner." And it was one of his greatest delights to look back upon the way by which God had led him. During his last affliction he was wholly confined to bed. "I was," says Mr. Miller, "his only Christian visitor;" and with what views and feelings the dying man regarded his visits, may be gathered from Mr. Miller's account of the last interview. It took place the night of Mr. F.'s death. "I called," says Mr. Miller, "at a late hour; after saying how pleased he was once more to see me, he added calmly, 'Remember all you do or say here to-night is for the last time, for I am a traveller about to depart, and I shall not return, but you may come to me. I have a true Friend with me; he knows the road, and I believe he will conduct me safely.' After reading the sacred word, I knelt in prayer with him and his family. During the exercise I was frequently interrupted with his solemn and repeated 'Amen,' 'Amen,' and on rising he took my hand and said, 'My dearest friend on earth, accept a poor sinner's thanks for all your kindness; you have indeed showed great care about my state. I attended Surrey Chapel for seven years, yet no one but yourself in all the congregation spoke to me, except the Benevolent Society's Visitors, who might think my profession was put on because of my illness or poverty ; but now, in a few hours, my sincerity is to be tested, and I bless God I have no fear about the matter, for God in Christ hath done all things well. On his arm I lean, and I glory only in him. Farewell, farewell! God be with you and make you a blessing to many.'" In a few hours after the "traveller" departed.

Another poor man, who, with his wife, had near twelve months before become members of the church at Surrey Chapel, and at this time lay upon his death-bed, said to him the day before his departure, after hearing of the end of Mr. F., "I, too, shall soon go to my Father's house ; and, sir, it is to you, as an instrument in God's hands, I owe my thanks ; but for you I should have perished in my sins,—I should have died a miserable being. The time was when I would have done anything that your visits should have been anywhere else. Many had come round before on Sundays with tracts, but I used to think they did not believe them themselves, or they would have been more determined. You evinced a determined mind. Neither my frowns nor my forbidding remarks used to daunt you, and God crowned your efforts with his blessing, not only to me, but to my wife ; and my prayer is, that you may long be spared to be a blessing to this neighborhood."

At the suggestion of the late Mrs. Sherman, ho next originated a class for the instruction of the Jewish children in the vicinity. Eight-and-twenty of these were quickly got together, from ten to eighteen years of age. They were met on Monday and Tuesday evenings, and instructed in the Scriptures of the Old Testament. They would listen with marked attention to tho history of the Hebrew patriarchs, and to any remarks upon their lives and characters. And sometimes, when they heard of their piety, they would give simple and affecting utterance to emotions of a religious nature. "Ah," they would say, "*we* do not attend to these things as we ought." Although not instructed in tho New Testament, they would voluntarily read in it, and, in fact, did of their own choice acquire a considerable acquaintance with it. In general they fully appreciated the instruction they received, and gratefully loved their friends by whom it was given. The class continued in operation for several years after its formation,—first under the superintendence of the late Mrs. Sherman, and subsequently of ladies connected with Surrey Chapel.

He had not unfrequently to meet with men hardly less fierce and extreme in their opposition than the savage hordes of New Zealand or Southern Africa, and even more intractable, yet he never shrunk from encountering, and rarely failed, by persevering kindness, to overcome them.

There resided in —— Place, a bigoted and violent

Romanist, who not only refused for many months to accept a tract, or to hear a word Mr. Miller had to say, but also, says Mr. M., " many times declared he would be the death of me if ever I came again into the court where he resided ; that if he saw me going to any of the houses he would drop something on my head as I passed under his window. But the more he threatened, the more determined I was to show him that I would visit all the people " Mr. Miller accordingly visited all the families, even those in the same house with himself ; " always, however," says he, " holding myself in readiness as I ascended his stairs for anything that might be done to injure me. On one of these visits I ventured to speak to him on subjects that I thought might be interesting,—as to the state of his health, and of the destitute poor, and began to think that I had got him into an earnest and friendly conversation, when all on a sudden he rose up, seized the poker, and made a rush at me. I instantly retreated down the stairs and was followed immediately by the poker, which my ungracious host had thrown after me. The next day I went again to see him. He seemed much surprised to see me again so soon. I said, ' I am afraid you were not well yesterday, or that you must have misunderstood what I said.' His wife, who was out the day before, asked what had taken place, and, on learning, became very angry with him ; and so I got an opportunity of speaking to him more at length, which I endeavored to do as affec-

tionately as possible" This in a great degree subdued him. He henceforth received Mr. Miller's
visits ; after some time, consented to unite with him
in the reading of Scripture and prayer; became himself a reader of the bible with which Mr. Miller presented him ; and was so eager for his visits, that they
could not too often be repeated.

The day of trouble is that in which especially the
minds of men are open to offices of real kindness,
and susceptible of ready, deep, and lasting impression, from religious teaching conveyed in the right
spirit. Then chiefly is " its season " And a kind
word spoken " in its season, how good it is." And
it is a great advantage of systematic and regular
domiciliary visitation by Christians, that it frequently brings them into contact with their more deeply
fallen fellow-creatures at such times, and establishes
beforehand, a perfect confidence in the genuineness
of their sympathy. How powerful *then* is the well-
known, though perhaps previously disregarded voice
of Christian kindness, to open the heart to religious
instruction, and how forcible then are " right words."
Nor was Mr. Miller wanting in aptness to speak " a
word in season to the weary." His own varied and
painful experience had effectually taught him how
" to have compassion" on the afflicted, especially on
such of them as were " ignorant and out of the way ;"
while his deep-felt concern for their spiritual welfare
and the cause of Christ, made him ever ready to
turn, if he might, their suffering to the account of

these. After calling in April, 1844, upon Mr.
R—— he says,—"As I entered the house I found
it to be the scene of mourning, for a melancholy accident had taken place only the day before. Mr. R.,
who was accustomed to amuse himself in the morning and evening of each day by a little carpentering,
had left some shavings strewed about the house;
and Mrs. R. having stepped into the next house to
assist a poor woman in her confinement, had left
their daughter with another little girl at home to
play." The shavings became the means of amuse-
ment for the children. Mrs. R.'s little girl having
decked herself out in ringlets taken from these, and
ascended a chair to gaze at herself as mirrored in
the glass above the mantel-piece, one of the loose
ringlets had caught the fire, and communicated it to
the rest, and in a moment lit up around her a fearful conflagration, in which she had perished. He at
once entered into their circumstances, threw his
heart into theirs, and sought, first, if not to impart
some consolation to their minds, at least to mitigate
somewhat the bitterness of their grief. "I endeavored to lead the minds of the broken-hearted parents
to look at the event under some less gloomy views,
and then went on to speak of the influence it should
have upon themselves. I spoke to them of their
state and condition before God, and of their duty to
attend to this as a solemn admonition that they too
must shortly leave this world, and ought to seek the
necessary preparation for a better. I read with

them portions of Scripture, and knelt in prayer. They appeared composed and thoughtful. They were led to look upon the awful death of their child as a solemn warning to themselves; both commenced attendance at the house of God, which they had wholly neglected, and sent their children to day and Sunday schools." Mr. R. afterwards stated, says Mr. Miller, that, "at any other time he could not have sat to hear what was then said to him, but would have put me out of his house; as it was, he regarded my visit as sent in the providence of God, and received my statements and admonitions with the meekness of a little child. He became hopefully converted to God."

The following is a more decided instance of the advantage thus gained. "Mrs. D., of —— Place, was a violent opposer of religion. For four years, I regularly called upon her without being able to obtain permission to read the word of God; more than once she put me out of the room, and in one instance did her utmost to throw me down stairs. Fortunately, I was more than a match for her in strength; had I not been, down I must have gone; notwithstanding, she stormed and raved until she drew a crowd of people around that filled the court, all of whom united to censure and denounce her conduct, and showed respect for me." At length, after four years' anxious and fruitless toil, he saw her health begin to decline. "I now," says he, "saw my opportunity, and carefully sought, by kindness, to com-

mend both myself and the word of God.   At last I
got her ear to the reading of that word.   I was afterwards permitted freely to visit her as often as I
pleased.   My visits became so prized that they
never could be sufficiently frequent and lengthy ; it
was my joy to see in her what appeared to be a
sound and decided change of heart.   She died professing, as a poor penitent sinner, to rest only in
Christ for salvation.   I am," adds he, "led to hope
well of her eternal state."

He was most sensitively alive to everything like
injustice on the part of one person towards another ;
had great sagacity and readiness in detecting it, even
where most artfully disguised ; the keenest and
deepest sense of its baseness, especially when at all
aggravated ; and the strongest compassion for those
who were its unhappy objects, particularly when
young and defenceless.   Such a case would at any
time instantly engage his sympathies, and call forth
all his energies, and it was in such cases that the
force and excellence of his character shone forth
most brightly. Here is an instance,—" Eliza W——,
a girl but fifteen years of age, had been brought before the Committees of the Southwark Female Mission and the London Female Penitentiary, as a fallen
girl, and, on the mere statement of her mother, had
been concluded to be such ; but, in consideration of
her age, she had been by them refused admission to
their institutions, it being deemed most advisable
that she should be under the care of her parents.

On this, however, a lady, a member of the former committee, sent her to me, in the hope that I should be able to get her into an asylum. But on my inquiring into the case, I found that there was no evidence to support the allegation, notwithstanding there could be no doubt but that she had been a naughty girl. I also found that the woman who had brought her was her stepmother, and that, whilst she preferred so grave a charge against this one, she spoke of her own three children as being all very good. This aroused my suspicions: I immediately felt it my duty to attend to the case for the protection of the child. My first step was to inquire into her character, and then see her father. I found that even her naughtiness was chiefly to be laid to the woman's charge, and that her father had too readily listened to the very unfavorable and false reports of his wife. This investigation took place in the presence of the mother, and it could soon be seen that I had more influence over the feelings of Mr. W. than she liked. I was concerned to avoid making unpleasantness between them, if I could; but at all events, I was resolved to do my duty. I appointed a time when I would see her in the evening, and engaged, in the meantime, to find a suitable asylum for the girl. This I did. But when I went to visit Mr. W., he was out, and was not expected home till very late. I felt that this was a deep-laid scheme of the woman, and said I would see him if I searched the parish round. I then called at

Lambeth Workhouse to see that the girl had been
taken there ; and, whilst talking with the matron, I
overheard a conversation between the two door-
keepers, which I thought I could turn to my account.
It was about that very girl. I said to the junior
one, ' Mr. Martin, you know that girl's father, don't
you ?' ' Yes, sir,' said he. ' You are going to have
a drop of gin with him presently, are you not ?'
' Yes, sir,' he said, with a smile, ' and my mate too,
as Mr. W. has been to see if you had brought her
here.' I said, ' I should like to go with you.' ' Very
well, sir,' said he, ' I will go now.' We went to a
public-house, where I saw Mr. W. very comfortably
seated to his glass of gin and water. I saw I must
now bring the matter to an issue. He at first said
he could not afford to pay for the girl's living in an
asylum. I said, ' Then put away the drink, for I
am resolved you shall know the facts of this case.'
I then entered into it with him, and he appeared
much affected ; fortunately there was no one in the
parlor but ourselves. He at length said, ' Well, sir,
if I live on two meals a-day, I will follow your advice ; and if you will take her to the asylum, I will
pay her expenses.' The Reformatory at Westcomb
Park, Maze Hill, Greenwich, is the only institution
of the kind which admits refractory young people
without their having received a magistrate's sentence ; I sought, therefore, for her admission into
this, and obtained it at the rate of six shillings per

week. The father went with me, and paid one month's charge in advance."

There was no description of usefulness he so much desired and rejoiced in, as that which has respect to the spiritual salvation of men, and there is no instance of this that appears to have afforded him more devout and grateful satisfaction than the one of which the following is an account. Mrs. N——— was a widow, with five small children. Mr. Miller was led to visit her through an illness, by which she was reduced to the brink of the grave. She was, at that time, not only a stranger to the influence of religion, but also was addicted excessively to drink. She received with great readiness and eagerness the instructions of her assiduous and friendly visitor, and earnestly sought to profit by them. " Sir," said she to him, on one of his visits, " a new thought has just come into my mind ; it is, that this illness is not unto death, but that you should be sent unto me, and that I should become what you have just described, ' a new creature' in Christ Jesus." She was restored to health, but continued to receive Mr. Miller's visits, and attend his meeting. " At my request," says he, " she attended my evening female adult school, where she learned to read and write." She also sent her children to the infant and Sunday schools, became regular herself in attendance on the public ordinances of God's house, and was at length admitted to communion with the church at Surrey Chapel. Amidst the cares and trials of a numerous

family, and circumstances of straitness and scar-
city, she continued exemplary in her Christian walk,
and was indefatigable in her efforts to lead others to
the house of God.   In three years from the time of
her own conversion, she was instrumental in leading
" eleven persons to sit beneath the sound of the gospel," and amongst them was " her own father, who
had been a most abandoned character," but became
through her completely reformed in his moral conduct, if not also the subject of a spiritual and saving
change.

The following is, in some respects, a still more
pleasing instance of usefulness of this description.
Mr. ——, of —— Place, had formerly been a pro-
fesser of religion, and a member of a Christian church
in the east of London ; but having removed his residence to this place had fallen into indifference as to
the obligations and blessings of religion, and the
means of grace.   Mr. Miller, on discovering this,
made it his business to arouse and reclaim him.
While addressing *him* his daughter, a young woman
of about twenty, listened with great attention, and
appeared to be impressed with the importance of
spiritual things.   " I invited her," says he, " to my
meeting ; she promised to attend it.   She did so,
and induced her father to accompany her.   They
continued to do this for some months.   They then
began also to attend a place of public worship.   When
I saw the father was satisfied with the minister
under whom he sat, and that he evinced a love for

the house and ordinances of God, I urged him to get his dismissal from the church to which he had belonged and seek an union with that with which he worshipped. His daughter said, ' I should like to join the church at the same time with my father.' " Mr. Miller inquired into her motives for this, and sought to elicit her true spiritual state ; and feeling satisfied with her reasons, and being persuaded of the reality of her conversion to God, he says, " I encouraged her to seek the union she desired." She did so, and the father and daughter were welcomed into the church together. This took place in October, 1843. In a monthly report for January, 1845, after referring to this event, he says, " I have now to record the more pleasing intelligence that the mother has been led to take the same steps." This now happy woman had been one of the most wretched slaves of drunkenness, and through her unhappy passion for strong drink had been a source of continual scandal and sorrow to her husband. " In one of her drunken fits," says Mr. Miller, "she scalded her hand, and had to be removed to an hospital. There I visited her. The word of God appeared gradually to make its way, and my visits were valued more and more. On her return home, I suggested to Mr. —— the duty and importance of family worship." This having been established, she afterwards highly valued, as having been a means of the greatest good to her. She also began to attend the house of God, and when she there saw her husband

and her child going to the table of the Lord, and
herself left to look on or go home alone, she became
distressed.   She felt her heart to be with them, and
that she could not endure that she should not be
altogether with them.   She made it a matter of
prayer, and was led to resolve on making a public
profession of religion, and seeking an union with the
people of God.   She is now a member of the same
church as her husband and daughter.   It is that
connected with the Independent Chapel, York Road.

Allusion has been made to his visits in the hospitals of the metropolis.   These abodes of suffering
and sorrowing humanity are singularly favorable
as fields for effective religious visitation, and most
desirable is it they should be fully and efficiently
occupied.   The afflictions of which their inmates
are the subjects, and those they behold around them,
tend powerfully to subdue the spirit, and to render
it serious and thoughtful, and specially susceptible
of deep religious impression ; while their separation
from the business and bustle of active life, the quie-
tude and silence of the place in which they lay, and
the solemnity of the events and doings which are
ever and anon taking place before them, greatly con-
tribute to strengthen this tendency—help to induce
this state of mind.   Welcome to the poor sufferers
within the walls of these dwelling-places of disease
and pain is the voice of sympathy, of kindness, and
of heavenly wisdom, and the presence of an earnestly pious and thoroughly Christian man, who will

"show unto them the way of life" How important and desirable that such should be abundantly provided for them. This at present is, in some instances at least, by no means the case. Each of them indeed has a chaplain, but is there always sufficient care that he is a man of the right description? After visiting in one of the wards of a principal metropolitan hospital, in October, 1844, Mr. Miller writes:—"There have been of late many, very many, important operations in the ward. Some have been followed by death. To the survivors I have been permitted to speak of the best things. They are in general very much pleased to have some one to speak with them freely and familiarly on these matters. Having directed their minds to Christ as the sinner's hope, one of them called me to her bedside, and said, 'There is some good to be got from that, sir; but I assure you the mummeries that the chaplain talks about are not worth hearing. A few weeks since he came up and said, when prayers were over, that on the day after he hoped he should see all of us that could go to the chapel there, as it was his intention to administer the sacrament, because it was St. Matthew's day, which ought to be celebrated as a holy day. In commemoration of him, therefore, he said, "We shall administer that ordinance, and, at the same time, I hope you will remember, that if you do not take the sacrament before you die, it will be utterly impossible for you to get to heaven; but, by this ordinance, all your sins are washed away."'

Such," remarks Mr. Miller, " is the doctrine of a chaplain of the finest hospital in London, and it will at once be seen how dark this place is." If the light —the only light—that is in thee be darkness, how great is that darkness !

Mr. Miller was under no official requirement to go to these " houses of mourning," and indeed was permitted to do so only in addition to his ordinary labors. It was of his own spontaneous choice that he visited them. Nor was it without great effort that he obtained access to them. The jealousy of chaplains, and the prejudices of other official persons, for the most part threw no small difficulty in the way. He, however, by prudence and perseverance, succeeded in inspiring confidence, in opening himself a way into almost all of them, and in some obtained permission freely to visit the patients. He sometimes met with cases in these noble institutions of a very remarkable character. Here is one :—" On the same day," says Mr. Miller, writing on Nov. 28, 1844, " there died in Lazarus' ward, Guy's Hospital, a wretched man, who would never suffer any one to speak to him on the subject of religion. To all appearance he was miserably poor. He professed to be unable to pay for being shaved, and actually begged a penny from another poor patient in the same ward for the purpose. His wife, who is a decent woman, and his children, of whom there were four, were all in the greatest distress. Yet, when he died, there was found about the person of the miserable man no less a sum than £31 8s. What a monster is such a being! The money was paid over by the steward of the hospital to his widow, who, as she received it, literally fainted with joy. I used this case,' adds he, ' in speaking to the rest in the ward, urging them to lay up treasure in heaven, where moth and rust do not corrupt, and thieves do not break through and steal."

All those to whom, in these kindly retreats of suffering, he could get access, he diligently sought to instruct and bless, yet ordinarily his efforts among them had special reference to particular persons to whom he stood in some way related. These he labored for with great assiduity and care, and was the means, in many instances, of leading them to enjoy a peace which the world cannot give, which " neither life, nor death, nor any creature" is able to take away. One only of these shall be mentioned. It is that of Mr. H——, of —— ward, St. Thomas' Hospital. This poor man, afflicted in body, was still more sorely troubled in spirit. His " sins had taken hold" upon him, "his iniquities had gone over his head." " He felt that he had done more evil than any one, that his sins exceeded those of every other person, and could not be pardoned." He had sunk into despondency, and a deep gloom had settled upon his spirit. " I sink in deep mire," he had to complain, "where there is no standing." " ' I am glad,' " said Mr. Miller, " ' that you see yourse'f in such a light. Had you not done so, I could not have offered to you the blessings of the gospel, or, at least, regarded you as in a state of mind to receive them. It is to sinners the gospel is sent, to the chief of sinners especially, and it is to them that its promises are given. And He has said, 'Let the wicked forsake his way, and the unrighteous man his thoughts, and let him return unto the Lord, and he will have mercy upon him, and will abundantly pardon ;' and Christ has said, 'The Son of man came into the world to seek and to save that which was lost.'" This last word fell into his heart—'lost!' exclaimed he, and the big tears rolled down his cheek. I knew not whether to regard them as tears of grief or joy, but as I continned to speak of the love of God, and of his willingness to pardon and accept the greatest sinner, a new light seemed to break in upon his soul, and his sorrow gave way to a rapture which cannot be described, and can only be known by those who have felt the same. I was not a little glad to leave him with such a light upon that countenance that had so long been covered with gloom."

While thus exerting himself, so far as he had opportunity, for the spiritual good of these sons and daughters of affliction, he sought also to enlist the agency of others in the same work, and thus indirectly to confer upon them the best blessings. So he uniformly endeavored to get the esteem and confidence of the sisters of the wards, and then to induce them to take charge of a quantity of tracts and to circulate them among their patients, and to point out to him the cases in which any effect was produced. This he succeeded in doing with many of the sisters, and the following is an instance of the success that attended this mode of operation :— "Visiting," says he, " in —— ward, Guy's Hospital, in 1844, I was told of a poor woman who was too ill to admit of any hope of her ever recovering, but of whose spiritual state the sister, a pious woman, hoped well. I hastened to her bedside, and had some conversation with her as to the world to come, and her prospects with regard to it, when she said, ' Oh ! it is of no use now to speak to me of those things ; it is too late. I shall die and be undone forever ; there can be no hope for me. No tongue can describe the greatness of the sins I have committed.' I directed her attention to various portions of the word of God, setting forth the freeness of salvation, and the readiness of God to pardon and accept the chief of sinners who come to him through Jesus Christ, and dwelling particularly on Isaiah lv. 6, 7, with which I closed. During the whole of this time she listened with an avidity which I shall not soon forget ; and when at last I paused, she cast her eyes upon me as if to see whether indeed I believed my own words, and then, with a look which cannot be described, feelingly and solemnly demanded, ' And *will he* save *me* ?' ' Yes,' said I, ' if as a poor sinner you come to him in the name of the Lord Jesus Christ.' ' I never could pray,' she proceeded to state, ' till I came here ;

since then, I trust, I have prayed in sincerity, thanks to that little tract which the sister lent me.' She lived but a few hours after, but was full of hope, and died praying like the holy Stephen, 'Lord Jesus, receive my spirit.' Thus," observes Mr. Miller, "is seen the importance of making friends of the sisters of these places, who will take charge of a few tracts, and judiciously lend them to the patients."

No description or degree of usefulness was thought lightly of by him, and no opportunity of doing good or preventing evil, in any form or measure, was overlooked or slighted. On one occasion, when visiting in Guy's Hospital, he was informed that a patient, who was pointed out to him, was about to go out that day, and should take the coach for her home in the country at four o'clock; but that a girl, whom he knew to be of bad character, had been with her, and had arranged to meet her, to take her in the evening to the theatre, and afterwards to her own home. He instantly saw in this a plot for her moral ruin, and took steps to defeat it. "I named the case," said he, "to the sister of the ward, who called the girl to me, in her own private room. As soon as the girl understood that the case was known to me, she said she had been very much troubled about it, but knew not what to do; as, if she went to the coach, the other girl would meet her there. I offered to see her safely off, when she burst into tears, and prepared to

accompany me.   I took her to the coach : the
other girl was there, but, as soon as she saw me,
ran off as fast as she could."

In the true spirit of a devoted Christian missionary, he identified himself, as far as he could, with
every institution and effort directed to arrest the
downward course of lapsed humanity.   So at an
early period he hastened to seek an union with the
Surrey Chapel Auxiliary to the Religious Tract
Society, and became one of the most efficient and
useful members of its committee.   In the same
spirit he immediately threw himself, though at a
distance from the scene of his labor, into the Sunday
Evening Ragged School, Jurston Street, Lambeth,
and never afterwards forsook it.   This school is said
to have been the first of the kind that was formed
in London, and, in many respects, has been one of
the most efficient and useful.   Here Mr. Miller was
engaged, first as a teacher, and then for three years
as the secretary.   And here, from Sabbath to Sabbath, with rare exceptions, when the "multitude
kept holiday," and "went up" together, with Sab-
batic tranquillity, to the courts of the Lord, he,
with a few others—"a band of men whose hearts
the Lord had touched"—were wending their way
to meet the most miserable outcasts of society, and
patiently to labor amidst heart-sickening scenes to
redeem these hopeless ones from utter ignorance and
vice.   As the secretary to this school, Mr. Miller
contributed greatly to its efficiency, and obtained for

it a degree of public consideration and influence it never enjoyed before.

He took a very lively interest in the case of poor and neglected youths, both in and out of the school; and never seemed more in his element than when seeking to snatch them from impending ruin. The following is an instance of this, and an example of one of his modes of operation on their behalf. Charles —— was a sharp and intelligent boy, and had received what, in the ordinary sense of the phrase, might be called a good education; but in all other respects, had grown up in almost entire neglect. His father, though an educated man, was an abandoued profligate; and his mother was, if possible, still worse. Mr. Miller induced the boy to attend the Jurston Street Ragged School. In September, 1843, Charles's father died. His degraded mother spent all she could in drink, and would often wake up her children at three or four o'clock in the morning to let her in. Poor Charles, destitute of care and support at home, also found himself unable to obtain employment abroad, and was sometimes reduced almost to desperation. "One Sunday night," says Mr. Miller, "while at school, this poor boy, having suffered much through hunger, said, 'Mr. Miller, if I don't get something to do soon, I shall make a hole in the river, for I can't stand it much longer' I remonstrated with him, and urged him still to try to get a place, 'Aye, it's all very fine, Mr. Miller,' said the boy, 'but you know what sort of characters we have in the neighborhood, and you know, if I got a place to-morrow, my mother would spoil it for me in a day or two.' 'Well, Charley, would you like to go to sea,' said I. 'Yes,' said he, 'and if you will only undertake to get me a berth, I will do anything you tell me!' I directed him to the Marine Society, and in a few days got him a letter of recommendation to the Committee." On the first meeting of the Committee, he was received and sent on board one of their ships. In three weeks after, he was bound apprentice on board an Indiaman, and sailed for China. "The day after his being bound, he called on me," says Mr. Miller, "in full sailor's dress to thank me, when, after a long conversation, he said he felt fully convinced that his going away in this manner would prevent his being either transported or hanged, for that he must have done something bad, had he stayed here much longer; and as he told me this, the tears streamed down his checks. I knew him to be fond of reading, and therefore presented him with a considerable number of tracts, and gave him such counsel as I thought would best suit his case. On leaving, he said, "Well, sir, I shall never forget you; and if I should live to come back from China, I hope I shall find you well, and that God will pay you for all you have done for my good.' "

In the same spirit he threw himself into connection with the Christian Instruction Society of Surrey Chapel; penetrated with them from time to

time, the miserable lodging-houses of the "Mint,"
and sought among the degraded wrecks of humanity
that so thickly strew these shores of life, cast hither
by its adverse or indignant heavings, to diffuse the
healing truths and influences of a living Christianity.
This Mint, as its name imports, is the place where
formerly the coin of the realm was made. It was
at that time inclosed by gates, within which many
families of distinction had their dwellings. The
residences of some of these continue to this day.
But "how is the gold become dim, and the fine
gold changed" The distinguished residents have
long ago vanished. The property, at a later period,
was thrown into Chancery, and the place became a
mart for the sale of furniture, a haunt and harbor
for abandoned women, and a hiding-place and strong-
hold for thieves. Gradually it has been drained of
its trade by the more attractive thoroughfare of the
New Cut, and left in the almost sole possession of
the dregs of society of every species. It would seem
as if formed on purpose to attract and accommodate
these. It is extremely close, is furnished with but
little more light than suffices to make darkness
visible, and abounds in dark and narrow courts. It
affords almost every facility for the protection of
thieves, and the concealment of their prey. Its
houses, in some instances, run one into another, and
have different doors for ingress and egress communicating with as many various streets. They are also
furnished with trap-doors and cellars. One of them

is distinguished as having long been the dwelling of the infamous " Jack Shepard." Such is the character of the people and the place that, before the establishment of the New Police force, no one would dare to pursue a thief within the gates. Once there, he felt himself, and was felt by all, as safe as if entrenched in the most impregnable citadel.

It is now occupied by about nine hundred families, generally numerous; and of these, in 1846, only twenty persons professed to attend any Protestant place of worship. There are in it upwards of thirty lodging-houses. It is difficult for any one not personally acquainted with these places, so abundant now in all the poorer parts of the metropolis, to form any fair and full idea of them. They differ in size —accommodating from ten to upwards of a hundred each. They are in general badly constructed, and worse conditioned. Most of them are kept by persons who themselves reside at a distance in the more aristocratic parts of the city, or in the suburbs, deriving from them an ample income, and living in comparative affluence and splendor. In some cases several are held by the same person, yielding them an almost princely revenue.* They are sometimes let to individuals at a fixed rent, to be re-let by them ;

* One man came to London a journeyman carpenter, with but five shillings in his pocket, but afterwards, in this way, realized upwards of £10,000. A single family has been found to hold a great number of these houses, and others, notoriously " *bad*," in different parts of the town, and to have

in other instances they are intrusted to deputies to be managed for the proprietors. They are, for the most part, subjected to the least possible restriction or regulation. Persons of almost every age, character, sex, and social grade, mix indiscriminately together. " I have seen," says one familiar with them, "the illiterate and the learned, the reckless spendthrift, and the child of misfortune, the broken-down tradesman, the artisan, and laborer, the mother with her babe and her children of a larger growth, and youths, fast shooting into womanhood and manhood, mixed promiscuously with fallen girls, abandoned women, and notorious thieves."

The modes adopted by them for obtaining a livelihood are very diversified, and generally very strange. There are beggars of numerous species, ballad-singers, sweepers of public crossings, costermongers, cabdrivers, tumblers in public-houses, jugglers, knobblers, or mobsmen, with their fancy women, street-walkers, and street-chalkers, highflyers or professional writers of begging letters, cadgers, and thieves of various hue and name,—as counter-jumpers, till-priggers, molbursers, whose business it is to dive their hands into ladies' pockets, &c.*

Here many of the deformed, limping, half-naked

accumulated the sum of £90,000 to £100,000. In one instance, in St. Giles's, both the proprietor and deputy were Roman Catholic priests.—See *City Mission Magazine*, August, 1845. See *Life of a Vagrant*, a resident in their midst.

* See *London Labor and the London Poor.*

impostors, who perambulate the streets of London during the day, and by a thousand deceitful arts extort from and rob the public, may be seen at night practically asserting their independency of their crutches, rejoicing in their freedom from the thraldom of their bandages, attired in their proper costume and exhibiting their true characters, regaling themselves extravagantly with costly meats and drinks, dancing to the voluptuous sound of music, or gambling and card-playing—their favorite occupation—uttering oft the most profane and filthy language, and engaging in the most savage and sanguinary combats, the walls resounding not unseldom to the shriek of terror and the cry of murder. Justly are they designated "the worst sinks of iniquity in the metropolis." No person can once enter them as an abode with impunity. He that ever crosses their threshold, to abide in them though but for a night, returns no more the same as he entered. Decency forbids even the mention of the gross and terrible abominations which, in some of them, are continually exhibited. Here youths of both sexes, some driven by the storms of adversity, and others fleeing from their deserted masters and mistresses, or hiding from their forsaken and broken-hearted parents, seduced and runaway children, servants and apprentices, are first placed in the midst of objects and influences that deaden every moral sensibility,—then drawn into the worst companionships,—then schooled systematically into professional vagrancy and vice, and become at length abandoned street-walkers, inmates of prisons, or tenantry of the hulks and penal settlements.

It was into these houses that Mr. Miller and his friends were accustomed, from time to time, on a Sabbath afternoon or evening, to carry the lamp of life. Here they read and expounded the word of God, sung his praises, distributed tracts, familiarly conversed, and otherwise sought to disseminate the gospel. The number in attendance averaged about forty. It was a strange and motley assembly, and odd was the spectacle exhibited by them on such occasions. Imagine the speaker, in the centre of a large mess-room; before him is a huge and blazing fire; around, on every hand, are benches and tables occupied by persons of the above description. Some are seated, some standing, some lounging or sleeping, some cooking, some eating, some smoking, some talking, criticizing the speaker, or what he says, and most unceremoniously dashing in and out of the room. But this is a favorable view: sometimes the scene was one of the wildest uproar. One of these is mentioned by Mr. Miller, under date of October, 1844. "I held (the day previous) a meeting at the —— Lodging-house. There were near forty persons. All went on very well, until a drunken woman came in—a noted beggar in the streets. As soon as she entered, she said she was not of my religion, so I should not preach there. The landlord appeared and tried to put her to silence, but in vain; for two men joined the woman, and were worse than she. The tumult rapidly increased. Obscenity and blasphemy rolled from their tongues like a torrent. Many regretted it, but could do nothing. I tried to proceed, but was unable, so I concluded by giving away some tracts."

There is a large number of persons scattered through society, who have at some time been members of Christian churches, and given evidence of decided piety, but have subsequently fallen away from the ways of God, and cast off all profession of religion, who are, notwithstanding, secretly wretched, and want but kindly to be smitten with the rod of truth, to become like the rock in Horeb, fountains of living water. One such case has already incidentally been mentioned, as associated with the labors of Mr. Miller Here is another :—" Mr. S——, an aged man, bordering upon seventy, was for many years a member of the Wesleyan body, but for the last seven has been a wanderer from the fold. From the first he gave a favorable reception to my visits, and even began to appear at my meeting. At the close of one of these he came to me, expressing a desire to have some private conversation with me, and requested that he might be permitted to call upon me for the purpose, as his daughter was always at his house when I called upon him. He accordingly came at a time I had appointed, and related to me his history with reference to religion. He is another example of open apostasy, arising, in the first place, from the neglect of closet prayer. Having finished the mournful story of his declension and fall, he added, 'But, my young friend, the Lord has not suffered you to come to me alone. Your appeals to the conscience have at times almost unmanned me. Your addresses at the meeting have been all to me. I have seen the time when I could not have sat to be talked to by one of your age. But now, sir, I thank God and you for your visits, and I wish now to say how I should like again to be numbered with the people of God, if you think proper I should be. But whatever you advise I will gladly do.' I gave him a letter of introduction to one of the members of the Methodist Society, Broadwall, who has since received him into his class : and the poor man says he feels at home again, and prays that he may stray no more."

The afflicted and the aged were amongst the objects of his special solicitude, and his visits of mercy to their cheerless abodes were joyously welcomed as the greatest privilege, and in many cases appear to have been a means of the highest good. Mrs. M——, of W—— Street, was the subject of great affliction. Through many weary months she watched and waited at the bed of an afflicted husband, whom at length she followed to his grave. He was "her all on earth," and bereft of him she saw herself alone in the wide world without a solitary friend, and encompassed with poverty on every

hand. Mr. Miller attended her in her trouble, unfolded to her the love of God in Christ, the blessings
and consolations of that love, and the way to their
obtainment. Welcome to her was the voice of
Christian sympathy and kindness which she heard
in him, and still more the tidings of heavenly blessing which he proclaimed. Those tidings she was
led to believe, and those blessings she was led to
seek and find. She made the Saviour her trust,
"and on him," says Mr. Miller, "her mind has
been stayed amid all her difficulties and troubles.
I am her only Christian visitor, and so she would
say sometimes, 'Oh, sir, until you came to me I was
a stranger to God and to all that is good; but now
I hope I can say, "The Lord is my light and my
salvation too."' After many fruitless struggles to
maintain herself, she found at length the attempt
was hopeless, and she was compelled at last to
accept the asylum of the workhouse. I saw her as
she returned from the relieving overseer with her
order for the house. She burst into tears and said,
'Oh, Mr. Miller, I do feel it very hard, after working all my life, to be compelled to go into the
house.' I said, 'Well, but, my friend, you will be
far more comfortable there than out, and I shall see
you each week, which is oftener than I can see you
now.' On hearing that she took up her apron,
wiped away her tears, and said, 'Do you visit
there?' 'Yes, every Friday,' I replied. 'Then,'
said she, 'I shall be content. God bless you.'"

In these secluded places, where there is so little to
diversify employment, or break the dull monotony
of life, the visits of a frank, sympathizing, and faithful man of God, are in general most welcome. His
words are listened to with no ordinary respect and
love. They are perchance the only words of kindness and of counsel which ever fall upon their ear,
and not a little glad are they to get hold of a fresh
and interesting tract from time to time, to fill up the
vacuum of life, to vary the dull beat of daily duty
or engagement, and to supply them with some matter of new and pleasing thought and conversation.
How eligible are such places as scenes of Christian
visitation! How full of promise and of hope to
those who lovingly enter, and well and wisely occupy them! How loudly is it called for by them;
how imperfectly enjoyed! The union house of St.
Saviour's had been perhaps in this respect provided
for as well as any, but not so well as to leave no
room for further help and effort. This Mr. Miller
perceived. Attracted by the necessities, not the
riches; the spiritual wants, debasement, and mise-
ries, not the temporal distinctions, splendor, and luxuries of these less favored children of earth, and less
successful competitors in the race for fortune, he
sought access to this place. And hither, with permission of the guardians, he resorted every Friday
afternoon, conversing freely and affectionately with
the inmates on the things that belong to their peace,
and circulating amongst them religious tracts and

books. Every week he distributed fresh tracts to the number of 300 or 400, besides the books he lent.

For four years he continued thus weekly to visit all the poor in that house, and deep was the interest he felt in this department of endeavor. In April, 1845, an event took place which brought him into a new and more important connection with them. The Rev. E. Newth, who for many years had, in conjunction with the morning chaplain of St. Saviour's, conducted religious service with the whole of the inmates, having to remove into the country, resigned his office. Mr. Miller had occasionally officiated for Mr. Newth, and was endeared to the poor by his affectionate and careful visitation of them ; and now that Mr. Newth was retiring, they united in the request that he would seek to succeed him. By their desire, and with the advice of some of the best of his own friends, Mr. Miller addressed the board of guardians on the subject, when the appointment was immediately given him. He commenced his labors on the 2d of May, and continued freely and diligently to perform them, addressing from 300 to 400 people with acceptance, from week to week, to his death. His benevolent exertions amongst these less favored partakers of our common humanity, were a means to some of the highest good. Here is an instance. " Mr. C—— is a blind man. He has long been the subject of deep conviction of sin and great concern for the condition of his soul. He says it is owing to what I have said to him on

these subjects from time to time. His great difficulty has been to know how so great a sinner could
be made fit to go to heaven, or could be forgiven.
I directed his attention at different times to various
portions of the word of God calculated to remove
this difficulty, and to guide him into the way of
salvation. God has been pleased to bless these instructions, and he is now, I believe, a possessor of
that liberty which is known only to the people of
God."

Another and more interesting case is recorded by
him. "When I first visited Mr. ——, in the St.
Saviour's Union, he was a stranger to all religion.
He had often heard me read in the ward, but, until
I distributed the tract 'All's Well,' he was a 'hearer
only.' He read this tract many times. The following Sunday he attended my meeting, for, as he afterwards told me, 'he could not rest' At length
he opened his mind to me, and desired to be directed
as to his uniting himself with the people of God. I
watched him closely for eighteen months, and finding him a consistent follower of Christ, I hesitated
not in advising him. He became a communicant at
St. Saviour's, as he preferred the preaching of the
Rev. J. Benson. But after this his career was
short. He was taken ill and removed to the infir-
mary, where I visited him. He was very anxious
to know that he was not deceiving himself. He had
many conversations with me on this point : at length
his mind became more and more fixed on Christ and

his word, so that, while he beheld in himself nothing but perfect weakness, he was enabled to cast away his doubts and fears. The influence of this man's piety was felt by many in the house, so much so, that some say now, when his name is mentioned, 'He was indeed a good man, though we had known him to be a very wicked man.' He was respected by all for his kind advice, and at times for rebuking the use of bad language. The last time I saw him, he said, 'If you never see any other good of your labors in this house, I hope you will be grateful, for God has made you the instrument in my conversion, and I hope you will have many more conversions.' In this peace of mind he died. His last prayer, I am told, was for the outpouring of the Spirit of God on my labors in that house; may that prayer be heard and answered."

During the summer months of each year he was accustomed, for the benefit of his health, to spend a portion of time upon the estate of that excellent Christian gentleman, the Hon. Captain Trotter, of Dyrham Park, during which he visited and conversed with the families and individuals resident or employed on the estate, held religious services, and distributed tracts amongst the laborers, who at this time of the year were very numerous; many of them Irish Romanists. These incidental efforts appear to have been highly valued by the people among whom they were put forth, and in some cases were greatly useful. Several examples might be adduced. Here

9

is one. Being on the captain's estate on Sunday,
June 1st, 1845, Mr. Miller held a meeting for prayer
and exposition of the Scriptures, which was attended
by upwards of 200 of these poor people. "The
morning following," says Mr. Miller, " I went to one
barn where there were about twenty-five Irishmen,
intending to engage with them in reading and
prayer. The day being wet was favorable to my
purpose. As I entered the barn it appeared completely dark. I stood in the light of the doorway at
which I entered, where they all could see me, and
said aloud, ' Well, my lads, I hope you are all in
good health this morning?' ' Ah, Mr. Miller,' shouted
out one at the top of his voice, from the more dis-
tant part of the barn, ' I have been thinking of
ever since, and if you will stop till I come do
will shake hands with you. God bless you! It is
this three or four years since I have seen you.' By
this time he reached the place where I stood, and
certainly if a tight grip and earnest shake of the
hand are any proof of affection, there was no want
of it in Barney Renegan. ' Now,' said he, ' my
lads, listen to him, he will tell you what is good,
and may God bless him that he may never want
bread.' " This odd and rude sort of introduction he
found to be of real service to him. "They were
most attentive while I spoke, and read, and prayed
with them, and afterwards united to pour forth with
overwhelming profusion their best and warmest
wishes for me. But Barney Renegan left the re-

id walked with me somewhat more than a mile,
lling me how he had been led to cast off Popery, and
hat persecutions he had had in consequence to en-
ire in Ireland, and how the New Testament I had
.ven him three years before, had been his constant
ompanion and comforter. ' I had,' said he affect-
igly, ' no other friend in the world.' "

When there, in February 7, 1843, he established
t the house of a farmer on the estate, a weekly
neeting for religious conversation and prayer, which
ontinued to be held for some years, and was some
vhat numerously attended.

The numerous member's of the captain's house-
old were the objects of his affectionate and assidu-
lorts, and there were those among them to whom
oors were a means of great and lasting good.
)t this the following letter, copied from one written
oy the French governess of the family, will afford
nteresting illustration :

"Dyrham Park, March 31.

"MY DEAR MR. MILLER,—I would have answered your
kind letter sooner, if I had not been prevented by the difficulty of expressing myself in English; but I will now put
aside all fear, and trusting in the Lord, I will try, hoping that
ou will forgive my mistakes. The reading of your letter
aade me very glad. I was pleased to see that, even absent,
ou continued to care for the welfare of my everlasting soul;
e therefore assured that I shall be most thankful for any
dvice and encouragement you may give me, and your letters
ways shall be welcome to me. Your departure left every
ne who knows you in sorrow; but it was the will of our
eavenly Father, and complaining would not only be useless,

but ungrateful towards him who provided so well for us during Mr. T.'s absence. We have every reason to believe that your residence among us has proved a blessing to some, as far as we poor mortals can judge; we think so, for since you came, there has been a change in some of the maid-servants. May the Lord grant his blessing on their efforts. I was very sorry not to have seen you before your departure. I had many things to ask you, but particularly to thank you for all the trouble you had taken in teaching us; God, in his everlasting mercy, will reward you for all you did, and all you do now for poor, sinful, perishing souls. Dear Mr. Miller, how often I wish I could have the opportunity of conversing again with you, of expressing freely what I feel, and what I want. My earnest desire is to live entirely after God's commandments, and to devote the remainder of my days to my Saviour; but there are many temptations within and without, and I feel I do not go on as I ought to do. I will be candid with you, dear friend, and tell you that I very often think that my faith is not the *true* faith; this thought makes me feel sometimes very miserable—tell me, is this thought a temptation of Satan? At other times I would not exchange the peace, the joy I found in my Redeemer for all the world could afford. Oh then, only then, do I feel happy; then is Jesus my Saviour precious to my soul—I love him above all, but *not enough.* I grieve, mourn over the coldness and ingratitude of my heart, particularly when I meditate on his wonderful love for us, and on his great sacrifice! Dear Mr. Miller, pray for me, pray for a new and contrite heart, a heart full of love for him 'who loved us.' You know what St. James says, ch. v. 16; your prayers must be answered. The texts of scripture you sent me are very comforting. They led me to examine myself, to see if indeed I was one of our Saviour's sheep, if indeed those beautiful promises are also for me. I would not deceive you nor myself, so I will tell you that some parts gave me great comfort, others distressed my mind, and made me think how very little I have done, till now, to show my love and gratitude to him who died for such a sinner as I am. If you knew, Mr. Miller, how God dealt with me, and what have been his mercies towards me —I can say, that in the furnace of adversity, his hand was leading me; whispering to my fainting heart, 'It is I, be not afraid.' Oh, his promise is ever sure.. John xiv. 18. I am rather afraid to tire you with such a long letter, but remember that you asked me to speak freely, and so I do. How are you now? Is your health better than when you wrote to me? May the Lord soon open the way for your removal from town. I assure you many are the wishes to have you near us; but we must wait the Lord's own time—he knows better. How glad I should have been to have met you in London, where I spent a few days. Do not be surprised if I stop you one day or another in the street; it is such a pleasant thing to meet a Christian friend, particularly in the Babylon you inhabit. Mrs. C—— sends her very best regards to you; we meet sometimes, for a little reading and prayer, and when we kneel down at the throne of grace, you are not forgotten

"With many thanks for your very kind note and advice, believe me, my dear Mr. Miller, yours truly in Christ,

"—— ——.

In the latter part of the year 1845, Mr. Miller was visited with much domestic and personal affliction, and was laid aside almost wholly for several months. But during this time an event took place for which he had labored long before without any apparent success—an event which now afforded him great delight, and which may encourage others to toil on even when no appearances of fruit may present themselves. There was a young man in the counting-house of his superintendent, who had obtained a strong hold of his affectionate sympathies. The young man had been respectably brought up, was of amiable disposition, and reputable moral character, but did not see that anything more was necessary. "I embraced," says Mr. Miller, "every opportunity of getting into conversation with him, and of throwing light upon his mind. At the same time, as I felt more than ordinary interest in him, and often grieved over his love of theatrical amusements and reckless waste of his property, upon these I made him the subject of many prayers." For more than two years, Mr. Miller continued thus to seek his good, apparently without effect. At length the desired change was brought about. Mr. C—— had been one Saturday night to a theatre, and the evening following, as it might have seemed by chance, he strolled into Surrey Chapel. The Rev. James Pridie, of Halifax, was the minister for the evening, and the text was, "Young men exhort to be sober-minded." What he then heard recalled all that his friend, Mr. Miller, had told him from time to time, and he felt that he could go on this way no longer. The day following he sought a private interview with Mr. Miller, and told him of the case. "It seemed," said he, "as if you had been telling the minister all about me, and it brought afresh to my mind all your conversation with me." "Like the stricken deer that seeks the shade," says Mr. Miller, "he came to pour out to me the anguish of his soul. We read, and conversed, and prayed together for several hours, during which he wept much, and seemed unwilling to leave me.

And when he heard that for more than two years he had been the subject of my prayers, he was greatly surprised and affected. ' No wonder, then,' said he, ' that I have been so unhappy in the theatre. How I could be esteemed worthy of your prayers I cannot tell; but I must look to you to be my friend, and whatever you may advise me, I shall be most willing to do.' He shortly after became a member of the church at Surrey Chapel, a diligent and efficient Sabbath-school teacher, and an active Christian."

He was at the same time gladdened with the report of another case, presenting a delightful triumph of long-protracted and apparently unavailing efforts. "In the year 1842 I first visited a family which was frequently the subject of great discord and strife. Mr. W——, the head of the family, is a good man, and, like Joshua, endeavors with his house to serve the Lord; but his mother, who lived with him, was strongly averse to religion; and hence came all their trouble. She could not endure the religious order of her son's house; always did her utmost to escape the pain of being present at family prayer. She finally left the house, and went to reside in the town of Macclesfield." Mr. Miller had frequently visited and expostulated with her, laboring to convince her of the sinfulness of her state, and to lead her to repentance, but apparently without success. While, however, at Macclesfield, the truth was made to take hold of her mind. She had escaped from the home and offensive piety of her son,

but it was only to brood over her own sir. and the
misery to which she was exposing her soul. She
was led, after some time, to a place of worship ; it
was an Independent Chapel. There her convictions
were deepened, and her trouble increased. "She
wrote," says Mr. Miller, "to me, telling me the
state of her mind, and asking my advice. I exhorted
her to continue in her attendance at the house of
God, telling her that I knew the minister, and com-
mending him to her. I also gave her such other
counsel and encouragement as I thought suitable to
her case ; and during my stay in the country, I was
comforted by a letter from her, in which she states
she has been received as a member into the church
under the pastoral care of the Rev. S. Bowen."

His was a district that literally swarmed with that
"curious race of human beings" so abundant in all
parts of the metropolis, known as the objects of
Ragged School philanthropy,—children and youths
who have been left, without instruction, restraint, or
control, to run wild upon the streets, exposed to
every wandering temptation, doomed there to eke
out for themselves a miserable subsistence, mostly
casual, always demoralizing, often criminal ; and,
consequently, lost in ignorance, vice, and misery, or
have been systematically trained to crime and infamy. They are indeed a remarkable race, " bold,
perty, and dirty as London sparrows, but pale, feeble,
and sadly inferior to them in plumpness of outline.
Their business, or pretended business, seems to vary

with the locality. At the west end, they deal in Lucifer matches, audaciously beg, or tell a touching 'tale of woe.' In the central parts of the town, Holborn, the Strand, and the regions adjacent to them, the numbers very greatly increase ; a few are pursuing the avocations above mentioned of their more Corinthian fellows. Many are spanning the gutters with their legs, and dabbling with earnestness in the last accumulation of nastiness ; while others, in squalid and half-naked groups, squat at the entrance of the narrow, fetid courts and alleys that lie concealed behind the deceptive frontages of our large thoroughfares. . . . . But it is in *Lambeth* and Westminster that we find the most flagrant traces of their swarming activity."

When, in the year 1844, the " Rookery" in St. Giles' was pulled down, large numbers of the most wretched and degraded people who had harbored there, crossed the Thames, and settled in the locality in which Mr. Miller labored, and its surrounding neighborhood. Many of these had large families, made up almost wholly of youths of the above description. The event thus contributed to swell prodigiously the number of these forlorn and miserable sharers of our common humanity who had previously abounded in the district. Within an area extending but little beyond the scene of his labors, there were 2,746 youths of this class at from 7 to 14 years of age, of whom 972 attended no school whatever, except the Sunday Evening Ragged School in the

neighborhood, with which he was connected, and
where the instruction given was, very properly, almost purely religious. But few of them attended
this. It is with reference to this, and other contigu-
ous parts, that the noble writer above quoted, says,
" There the foul and dismal passages are thronged
with children of both sexes, and of every age from
three to thirteen. Though wan and haggard, they
are singularly vivacious, and engaged in every sort
of occupation but that which would be beneficial to
themselves and creditable to the neighborhood
Their appearance is wild ; the matted hair, the dis-
gusting filth that renders necessary a closer inspec-
tion before the flesh can be discerned between the
rags which hang about it, and the barbarian freedom
from all superintendence and restraint, fill the mind
of a novice in these things with perplexity and dis-
may   Visit these regions in summer, and you are
overwhelmed by the exhalations ; visit them in
winter, and you are shocked by the spectacle of hundreds shivering in apparel that would be scanty in
the tropics. Many are all but naked. Those that
are clothed are grotesque ; the trousers, where they
have them, seldom pass the knee ; the tailed coats
very frequently trail below the heels. In this guise
they run about the streets and line the banks of the
river at low water, seeking coals, sticks, corks, for
nothing comes amiss as treasure trove. Screams of
delight burst occasionally from the crowd, and leave
the passer-by, if he be in a contemplative mood, to

wonder and rejoice that moral and physical degra-
dations have not yet broken every spring of their
youthful energies."

Many of them are without any home, and never
know the luxury of a bed ; many others have none
but the wretched lodging-houses. And any who
have retreats of their own, are found, when traced
to these, to be encompassed with every form of evil
that can offend the sense and deaden the morals.
These chiefly are the ranks from which our prisons
are replenished from time to time, and our penal
settlements peopled. They live mainly by begging
and stealing. Mr. Miller had long contemplated
the condition of these swarming outcasts with amaze-
ment and distress, and had looked in vain around
him for some means of rescue. He particularly
wished to obtain for them the advantage of some
general education, such as their age and circumstances would admit of their receiving. But how
to do this, was the difficulty. Filthy, ragged, dis-
eased, and crime-worn, their personal appearance,
apart from everything else, would prevent their admission to any British or National schools, and cut
them off from all hepe of education, except through
schools specially adapted to their case, and exclu-
sively confined to them. Mr. Miller having been
accustomed, for some years, to take a leading part
in the Sunday Evening Ragged School in Jurston
Street, had seen much of the working of such institutions, and acquired considerable fitness to conduct

them.   He accordingly determined to establish " A
Week Evening Ragged School for Youth of both
Sexes," but for purposes more comprehensive.   The
difficulties of s'ich an undertaking, under his circumstances, were very great, and required vast moral
energy and perseverance to overcome.   These he
fairly surveyed and fully estimated, but did not for a
moment shrink from.   " Gigantic," wrote he, " as
this plan may appear, I feel persuaded that I have
only to begin the work in a spirit of faith and prayer, and the mountain will disappear."   For several
months he was engaged in seeking a suitable place
for it, without being able to find one satisfactory to
himself.   In the meantime, " I was favored," says he,
" with the company of the Right Hon. Lord Ashley,
who for some days visited with me from house to house,
and from room to room, in one of the most wretched and inhospitable parts of my district, and witnessed scenes of the most revolting and heart-rending
description.   At the close of one of these days, as his
lordship sat in my house and spoke of the scenes he
had beheld, I mentioned my project of a week evening school for the neglected youth.   His lordship
immediately said he would do all in his power to aid
me in it, and accordingly, in a few days after, he
met at my house several ministers and gentlemen
whom I had invited to consult with him on the
matter, when the following resolution was passed
unanimously :—' That from the statement just made
by Mr Miller, City Missionary of Broadwall, it is

the opinion of this meeting that a week evening school for ragged children in this locality is needful and practicable, and that we form ourselves into a committee to carry the same into effect, and that three gentlemen be appointed to look for suitable premises in which to commence operations.' "

This latter business, however, almost wholly devolved upon himself. His infant school was then held in one part of the upper room of a large erection, chiefly of wood, in Broadwall, the lower story being out of use and unfit for any. At his suggestion this place was chosen, and to fit it for the purpose contemplated, it was subjected to very extensive alterations. The improvements were made chiefly under his personal direction, and the bulk of the costs, which amounted to about £30, was provided for by his exertions.

The alterations were completed with all possible expedition; in the meantime excellent teachers had been found by him; and on the evening of the 13th July, 1846, the school was opened. Crowds of dirty, ragged, bold, and reckless youths, far exceeding every expectation, presented themselves as candidates for admission. Only a part of them could be taken in; seventy of each, boys and girls, being deemed as many as could be at first efficiently instructed and governed by two teachers. Those admitted were accordingly restricted to this number. A strange and motley group they were; the pencil of Hogarth only could do justice to the pathos and the humor of the spectacle they formed. Many of them had been the frequent inmates of prisons, some, of almost all those in and about the metropolis, but were, with reference to the discipline of these, emphatically

"Worse for mending, washed to fouler stains."

Some were from the worst dens of infamy, kept by their own parents, and some were themselves its victims,—at once the offspring and devotees of shameless impurity. Some were the children of convicts, and in the way too likely to occasion their becoming such themselves; many were orphans; a large proportion subsisted by what they got upon the streets, as costermongers, vagrants, thieves, &c. And yet there was about them something interesting and hopeful. The girls were maidenly and modest in their demeanor, and the boys had vivacity and kindly humor. It was evident they regarded the idea of their going to school as forming matter for "fine fun." On the evening when opened, the boys and girls were for a short time assembled in the same room, and, after being duly instructed about what was proposed to be done for them, and what would be expected from them, they were addressed by their newly-installed master on the subject of *obedience* Cunning glances were rapidly interchanged in all directions, every variety of imaginable grimace was exhibited,—now and then a good-natured jest was uttered, commonly at the master's expense, or a strange antic performed; and in a few instances attempts were made to upset all order and turn the business into fun. After several unsuccessful essays at this, one bold fellow sang out " at if I had a donkey vot vouldn't go,"—and the whole mass burst into a loud and wild laugh. The master paused, and then said,—" Well, now, suppose you had a donkey what wouldn't go, and you had a load of corn to carry to a given place, and you found yourself in consequence conquered, would that be right in the donkey?" " No, sir," answered every voice " Certainly not," said the master; " and I hope that young man does not mean to compare you to donkeys. I should be sorry to do so, for you have minds that can think and reason,—you have souls that will not die,—and my desire is, to lead you to exercise those minds, and to learn the value of your souls. But let me here just say, you must not look on the donkey as being everywhere that stupid and unmanageable sort of animal which the cruelty of Englishmen has made him. If he is well fed and regularly cleaned, he is a pretty and useful creature. In some countries, even princes would think it no disgrace to ride upon one; and if you and I become more acquainted, I shall be able to tell you of a Prince of princes who rode on one. But now, to come back to the point we had in hand, there is the donkey and the load to be carried, and this young man wants the donkey to go; tell me what is to be done." " Why, hold a bunch of carrots before his nose, to be sure," responded one, drily. "That," said the master, "would be very kind of you ; and you may depend upon it, that donkey would like it much better than the broomstick, such as many beat and torture him with ; and I am very much obliged to that youth for the bunch of carrots, and it is my intention to hold out to *you* such inducements as may lead *you* to continue under my care until you know the value and importance of instruction ; so now, my boys, follow me into our own school-room." " This is a jolly good cove, aint he ?" said the lads, good-humoredly, as, with many strange grimaces and antics, they moved off after him. " I shall like this school."

But it was not always in such mild and manageable forms that their disorderly tendencies and eccentric dispositions showed themselves. There were a number of Irish lads who had, on some account, conceived a feeling of hostility towards the rest, and entered into a conspiracy against them. They had determined to fall suddenly upon their supposed enemies, on leaving school, and had furnished themselves with short sticks, which they attempted to conceal beneath their clothes. Thanks to their tattered garments, this device failed ; for, from beneath the garb of some, whose jackets had long before taken leave of their sleeves, and, in fact, were but the ragged remnants of their former selves, the sticks looked out and told tales *in* school. These unsightly weapons, thus unluckily protruding from their worn-out scabbards, quite defeated their wicked plot, and gave occasion for a wholesome lecture on "peace." Notwithstanding, a second attempt was made soon after ; although in this instance the viper was killed before it was fairly hatched, it was deemed desirable in future, for a limited time, to secure the presence of a policeman. It happened, fortunately, that the one obtained was a young man of kindly disposition, and of some sympathy with the work, he having been accustomed in previous years to teach in a Sabbath-school : he accordingly took a lively interest in the operations of the boys and girls,—sometimes hearing them read, and then helping them in their sums, and so the lads, out of very respect and love, called him the " King of the Peelers."

Degraded as these poor outcasts were, and fallen, as they seemed to be, even beyond help and hope, they were by no means entirely destitute of a sense of the importance of instruction. One poor boy, being observed for several nights to sleep, was asked how it was. " I think," said he, " it's 'cause I gets up so early in the morning." "At what time do you get up, my boy?" he was asked again " At four o'clock," was the reply. " And why do you get up so soon ?" " 'Cause I sells watercresses, and if I didn't go at that time I couldn't get 'em."

Of the privations to which these hapless youths are subject, few have any idea. Perceiving two boys much taken up with something, and apparently at play, the master called upon them to give up the

10

playthings to him ; they put into his hand a short pipe and a small paper of tobacco. They were but thirteen years of age. " Who gave you these ?" said the master " I bought them, sir," was the re- ply. " Why, do *you* smoke, R—— ?" The little fellow colored up, and said, " Yes, Mr. C——." " On putting it upon the mantel-piece," says Mr. Miller, " I said to a young man near me, one of the scholars, ' Who would think that that little fellow smoked ?' 'They have that,' said he, 'instead of wittles. When they are at the water-side, and have no grub, they smoke instead of eating.' " These poor boys were what they call mud-larks, a descrip- tion of youths who are accustomed to attend at the river-side on the ebbing of the tide, and wade into the mud in search of coals and other store that chance may have thrown in the way, and who de- pend upon these acquisitions for their support.

Notwithstanding their great and manifold priva- tions, they were not unwilling to pay for the advan- tages of education, so far as they could. Many of those who wished to write, very readily paid for their own copy-books ; and a considerable propor- tion of them, when informed by Mr. Miller that the Ragged School Union would sell them Bibles for 6*d*. each, and that they might subscribe for them in the smallest sums, as they might be able, immediately gave in their names. " I'll have one," said one girl before all the rest, lifting up at the same time her halfpenny in her hand ; " put my name down,

sir." Her mother was the keeper of a house notorious at once as a harbor for young thieves, and a
retreat for abandoned girls.

All that was first attempted or contemplated in
this school, was to give instruction in a kindly and
attractive manner to these wretched objects, in reading, writing, and arithmetic, in the Sacred Scriptures, in religious and moral truth, and other
branches of human knowledge, as far as might be
practicable. But there was subsequently introduced
a new and important arrangement, intended practically to train them to the habit of industry, and to
an acquaintance with certain useful kinds of handi-
craft. The girls were taught plain needlework, and
the boys tailoring and shoemaking. Classes were
formed for instruction in each of these arts, and
competent persons engaged to teach them. By the
end of the first half-year after their formation, it
was announced that " the tailors had made numerous caps and several pairs of trousers, the button-
holes only being the work of their teacher ; and that
the shoemakers also, had made surprising progress."
An incident is given in the first annual report illus-
trative of this. It was Mr. Miller's practice to obtain for the school, as far as he could, gifts of cast-
off clothes, first, as an exercise, to be repaired by the
scholars, and then to be given as rewards for industry and good conduct. They were found more eligible for this purpose even than new garments, inas-
much as they could not be pawned by their friends,

as those not unfrequently were, for mere drink. One
of these gifts deserves notice. A gentleman having
previously, within a few days, presented the school
with three parcels of east-off clothes, called at the
secretary's house with a fourth thus humorously en-
dorsed—

> "I leave at Mr. Miller's door,
>   My clothes' donation number four.
>   One ragged shirt, two ragged stocks ;
>   Some ragged gloves and ragged socks,
>   One ragged coat to warm the cool
>   Of ragged boys in th' ragged school ;
>   But not so bad—a stitch or two
>   Is all they want to make them do.
>   Wishing all happy, I remain,
>   Their humble servant, Joseph P."

In one parcel there were sent, among other things,
a pair of boots, which were afterwards given to one
of the boys to mend. Mr. Miller perceiving him
doing his best at soling and heeling them, and mistak-
ing them for a pair of his own he had given, promised the boy a shilling towards a new pair for himself in case he should "finish them nicely ;" Mr.
Miller intending to wear them as a proud trophy of
success in this dear department of his labors. They
were satisfactorily completed, cleaned, and put upon
the shelf, to await an occasion worthy of them. But
when the occasion came, and he attempted to put
them on, he discovered, to his sore disappointment,
that they were not his. They were afterwards
found to have been sent as a gift to the school by

that devoted and valuable friend of the ragged juve-
niles, Joseph Payne, Esq., barrister-at-law. To him
they were accordingly forwarded, with the history
of the case; he readily paid the cost, and subsequently, on great ragged-school occasions, with honest pride and pleasure, wore and esteemed them as
the substantial badges of a moral triumph far more
exalted than any achieved by the warrior's sword.

The girls, also, were very assiduous in *their* department, and soon learned to turn out well-made
garments with considerable despatch. Lord Ashley,
in an article already adverted to, referring to this
school with a view particularly to this peculiarity in
its arrangements, observes :—" We may describe one
lately established as a sample of the extension and
improvement which we may generally anticipate.
The system is that recommended by the British and
Foreign Society. The studies begin with Scripture
lessons, are carried through all the gradations of
the primer, slate pencil, and Cocker, aided by a
variety of attractive illustrations, and end with a
hymn. This is the ease four nights of the week, and
on the fifth (and here is the new feature) the children having commenced as usual, are disposed of in
industrial classes; the girls to every kind of needlework, the boys to the crafts of tailoring and shoemaking. Admission to the industrial classes is treated
as a reward, none being allowed to join them who
do not present a ticket as an evidence of their regular attendance during the former days of the week.

The number present on the last evening of which we have a return, were 63 girls and 42 boys, all brought from the most miserable localities. All were diligent and well pleased with the notion of mending their own clothes. A bargain was struck between the two classes of lads, that the tailors should mend coats for the shoemakers, and the shoemakers return the compliment to the tailors. Though the number which have been admitted into the school amounts to 283, yet the average attendance, such is the spirit of rambling, goes no higher than 53 boys and 71 girls. The school is open from half-past six to nine o'clock.

" The expenses of this establishment," continues his lordship, " are moderate ; the entire cost, including wages to master-tailor, master-shoemaker, and mistress of the needle-girls, being only about three-pence a week for each child, on the average attendance of 124, and not much more than a penny on the full complement of those admitted."

" Since the above was written," says Mr. Miller, writing a few months after, " the school has made great advances. Each youth is now permitted to purchase clothes in the school at half the cost price of the raw materials, and such is the influence that arises out of this, that boys to purchase a shirt or a pair of trousers, and girls to obtain frocks and under garments, bring all the money they can get, even their farthings, and at the present time there are not less than 108 different garments being paid for by as many scholars. The privilege is confined to the young people actually attending the school, and the plan is found to be much better than that of giving the clothes. The small shop-keepers in this district who sell sweetmeats, now complain that the scholars spend no more money with them."

It ordinarily took no very short period to complete a purchase, and not a little glad were the poor urchins if by any unexpected good fortune it was hastened. One boy had given his name for a shirt and paid towards it a penny, and there stopped for some time ; one day, at length, as he entered the school-room, he exclaimed, " Here is sixpence ; that is ALL for my shirt, and will pay for it." " How did you get the sixpence ?" said Mr. Miller. " A gentleman asked me to hold his horse, sir ; I did so a good while ; and when he came out he could not find any halfpence, so he said, ' Never mind, here is a sixpence for you,' and drove off. So it was a slice of good luck for me, sir."

Within six months there was paid by them into the school fund, for garments, the sum of £1 10s., which would have been spent in useless and hurtful trash.

" I just add," says Mr. Miller, " that seventy-three of the scholars have purchased bibles, most of which have been paid for by farthing subscriptions, and eighty-four have paid for their own copy-books."

An attempt had been made also, at an early period in the existence of the school, to teach them scientifically to sing. One evening of each week was ap-

propriated to this purpose, and lessons were given,
and exercises conducted, on Mr. Hullah's system,
under the superintendence of an efficient master ;
and it is surprising what progress these rude, untu-
tored, barbarian youths, who seemed to have no
" music in their souls," made in this pleasing, purifying, and ennobling art.   It was delightful to witness the manner in which they chanted various portions of the Church Service : it would not have dis-
graced the orchestra of the proud cathedral-pile of
the world's metropolis.

It was one of the objects contemplated by Mr.
Miller and his friends in the formation and management of this school, to promote the introduction of the
scholars received into it who behaved themselves
well into situations in which they might honorably
support themselves.   This object to some extent was
accomplished, and very gratifying was the evidence
supplied, by the way in which the youths filled
those situations, of the efficiency and excellence of
the institution in which they had been so generous-
ly taught.   A lady who, on visiting the school, was
led to take two of the girls into her service, kindly
engaging to give them, for their encouragement, each
£6 per annum, afterwards wrote to a member of the
committee the following pleasing testimony of their
worth :—

" My Dear Sir,—I have much pleasure in informing you
that the two girls I took as servants from the Broadwall
Ragged School are going on very well.   Their willingness

and anxiety to oblige more than compensate for any ineffi-
ciency in their work, and I prefer them much to the gene-
rality of servants to be had in the usual way. I have not
detected them in any falsehood, and there is a willingness to
attend divine worship which I am much pleased with.

'I remain, dear sir,

" Yours very truly,

" To Lient. Blackman, R.N."

Thus were his fondest anticipations, in connection
with this great undertaking, more than realized;
and affecting demonstration was given of the sound-
ness of those views in which it had originated, and
which are so truthfully and beautifully expressed in
the lines of Louisa Stuart Costello, on " Ragged
Schools," a copy of which was found treasured up
among his select papers.

" In the depth of a forest, dreary and dark,
  The traveller welcomes the glimmering spark
  That bids him press onward through labyrinths dim,
  For Hope, in the vista, is shining for him.
  His robe may be miry, his sandals be torn,
  His aspect be haggard, his features be worn,
  And some at his bearing may start in amaze
  And fear to approach him, and shudder to gaze;
  But tend him, and nurse him, the future will show,
  In the traveller rescued, nor brigand nor foe.
  'Twas but toil and fatigue that had clouded his brow,
  Still the light was within, and shines brilliantly now.
  In misery's world there are beings who stray,
  With no beacon to cheer and encourage their way;
  They are squalid, unnurtured, despised, and forlorn,
  And the polish'd pass by them with loathing and scorn.

But let the door open, and welcome them in,
Let the work of their rescue from evil begin
Be they taught; be they fed, and a gleam will yet shine
. To prove in their nature a part is divine.
The torch may be turn'd towards earth, but the flame
Rises ever to heaven—for from heaven it came."

Very much against his own wish, his oldest boys made choice of a sea-faring life. Unable to prevent this, he sought to turn it to the account of his usefulness. Availing himself of their agency, he endeavored, through religious tracts, to diffuse the knowledge and influence of the gospel on the seas, and learned from his eldest son that, on a foreign shore, English seamen would receive and read English tracts with the utmost avidity. On Thursday, 19th February, 1846, going on board the ship in which Robert, his second son, was to sail, he was invited by the captain to tea with him. "In the cabin," says he, "I found three other captains, whose ships lay alongside. After tea they proposed a hand of cards. At first I was at a stand what to do, whether to retire or to protest against the practice. I resolved on the latter, and succeeded in getting them into a conversation on religious subjects. Card-playing was a principal topic; I expatiated at length on the evil of this practice. One of them, in a very triumphant manner, said he supposed I did not know how to play, and that that was my way of getting out of it. I said, ' My friend, I am sorry to say, if I were disposed to play, I should be man enough to play you a hand at any game you might choose ; but I have a better card to play, and I should be glad if you would join me.' I continued to speak of the evil of the practice, when one of the captains said, ' Mr. Miller, you are a stranger to me, but you might have known my history. I have been twenty-two years captain, and had, after bringing up my mother's family and supporting one of my own, saved £300. But I began about two years ago to keep company and play at cards, and now, if I were to die this night, I have not a shilling to leave my wife and children, and it has all gone in this way ; and the other day, when I read a tract given to my mate by your boy, I thought I should have gone out of my mind.' At this statement, made with much feeling, the other captains seemed deeply moved ; and shortly after they said to me that they always looked upon Captain C—— as a man of considerable property. They all accompanied me ashore, and, on taking leave of me, promised me they would abandon card-playing, read their Bibles, and attend a place of worship when they could. I promised regularly to supply them with suitable tracts for their ships, and subsequently obtained a grant of ten shillings' worth from the Religious Tract Society for immediate use amongst them." He afterwards visited the vessel several times when it was in the Thames, distributing religious tracts, and conversing with the crew, and ultimately established in it a loan library, obtained by him as a grant from the Religious Tract Society. Through this he also got on board the rest of the vessels in the same trade, of which there were seven, and, besides circulating numerous tracts from time to time, established in each of them a similar library.

In the course of his labors, he sometimes met with instances of ignorance concerning sacred things, such as would hardly be credible to those who are accustomed to look upon society only in its brighter and better aspects, and was the means of leading its unhappy subjects to that knowledge which is "life eternal." Such was the case in reference to Mary S——. She was a young woman of about eighteen, of some personal beauty, and, generally, of a very prepossessing appearance. "When," says Mr. Miller, "I first called upon the family to which she belonged, I found her in a bad state of health, and, as I thought, not likely to get better. I soon discovered she had not been in a place of worship for many years. She was a quick-minded person, and in some matters rather intelligent, but was so ignorant as to religion that she was wholly unacquainted with the name of Jesus Christ, except as a byeword and as it is used in bad language. She knew nothing of the history or character of the Saviour, or that there was anything sacred connected with his name. I read a portion of the word of God to her. She said she had never heard it before, and had never before heard anything read out of that book, and that such things as it contains were never talked of in their family. I felt much affected with her case, for she was in many respects an interesting young woman. I gave her a Bible; she read it with great attention, and drank deeply of its interesting contents." He also personally visited and instructed her with great care and assiduity during the period of her sickness, expounding to her the Scriptures, and teaching her "the way of the Lord more perfectly." She soon came to look upon him as her best earthly friend, and to give the most earnest attention to the things she heard from him from time to time. "On the first day of her getting out," says Mr. Miller, "which was Sunday, she went to Surrey Chapel, and was much delighted with the service, and there she continued to attend regularly from Sabbath to Sabbath, till she returned to the situation she had left on account of her illness. Before returning, she called at my house, thanked me warmly for all I had done for her, and said she hoped I would pardon her, if she should call upon me at any time when she might be at home. I warned her of the temptations to which she would be exposed, supplied her with a select packet of tracts, and commended her to God in prayer. She has since called upon me twice, and I am pleased to find, that though she has much to contend with, both from the family she lives in and her fellow-servants in the house, she continues steadily to attend New St. Pancras' Church, and to hold fast her Christian profession."

It was about this time a case came full under his notice of the most revolting character, but which occasioned an interesting display of his characteristic benevolence, courage, fortitude, and strength.

"Mr. —— is a cabinet-maker, a good workman, and might always be employed, but is, together with his wife, an abandoned and notorious drunkard. He is, in consequence, so ragged and filthy in his person, that hardly any master will have him on his premises. His wife is like himself. She is commonly sitting, when at home, in one corner of the fire-place. The floor of the room, which is never washed, is covered with a thick coat of the most offensive filth, and the children, of whom there are five, the day long play in a state of nakedness about it. I have visited them for two years. I have often read to them the word of God, but have encountered from them much opposition. In June last, as my wife was in the act of locking the street door, before retiring to rest, she heard repeated cries of 'Murder,' from a boy, who seemed to be almost mad with fear. She opened the door and inquired for the cause. 'Oh! Mrs. Miller,' exclaimed he, 'my father has killed my mother—he has split her head open.'

On hearing this, I put on my coat and hat, and hastened to the spot. I found all the people up and at their doors, and the policeman at the top of the place, dreading to go down alone, and absolutely re-fusing to do so, until some other officer should come to accompany him. I went down to the house and, on entering the room, saw Mrs. —— in a state of nudity from head to foot, and covered with blood. The other four children were running wildly to and fro in the room. Finding she was able to pace the room, I immediately withdrew from the revolting scene. In vain did I ask any of the women living in the adjoining house to go into her. 'She may die,' said they, 'and be d——,' and so refused to go. I returned home. I found my wife at the door, anxiously waiting to see me come out of the court in safety; as I was telling her of the case Mr. —— passed, in company with a prostitute and two young thieves, all of whom I knew well. I said, 'Mr. ——, why don't you go home, and try to make matters all right with the old woman, and not go on in this way?' He said, 'My wife is mad, and not fit to live.' I replied, 'But that is no reason why you should be her executioner; come along with me, and see what is to be done.' To this he said, 'Well, I'll go, if you'll go with me; but I won't go alone.' 'Come, then,' I said, and together we went. All this time, the policeman had stood at the entrance of the place. The moment the infuriated woman saw us enter the room, she sprang forward, intending to seize her husband; but he, being aware of her, stepped out of the room in an instant, when she seized me by the collar of the coat with both hands, declaring she would have my heart out before I left. The blood was streaming from her head profusely, and I must say I began to be somewhat alarmed, for by this time she had become so infuriated, that she knew no one.   But at this moment, three of the most abandoned women got into the room and forced her from me ; while two others pushed me into another room on the same floor, and I thus escaped unhurt.   On returning home I went to bed, but not to sleep ; for as I lay, I thought of the state of the poor creatures, and how that Sabbath-day would be spent, that had been thus begun.   I could not help weeping for the sins of my wretched neighbors.   On the following morning, before going to my place of worship, I went to see them ; I could not rest content until I had discharged this duty.   I looked on them as objects of pity, and felt that it is only by the grace of God that I am made to differ.   The wretched woman was up, and when she saw me come into the room, she turned her head away from me, for she was ashamed to look me in the face.   I said, ‘ How are you this morning ?   I was truly sorry to see you in such a state a few hours since.’   She said, ‘ Mr. Miller, I am ashamed to look at you.   I am ashamed of myself.   I never could have thought that you would have come here again, and so soon too.’ I said, ‘ My friend, the reason I came is because I pity you, and would gladly do anything I could to bring you to a better state.   Pray tell me how did you get the wound in your head ?’   She said, ‘ My husband did it by throwing a ginger-beer bottle at me, in which we had some rum he brought home.

He had been at work all the week, and we quarrelled because he would not give me any money for food, which neither I nor the children had tasted all day. This, and the wound in my head, probably were the causes of the rum having such an effect upon me; and what, again, made me worse, was that I saw he was going with —— and ——, and you know what they are.' During all this time the husband lay asleep on a few dirty shavings, in a corner of the room." This family afterwards removed to some other locality, and were lost sight of. We know not, therefore, what may have been the results of his labors in their case.

During the latter part of the present year, he was again visited with a long succession of painful domestic afflictions. For three months, his wife was compelled by indisposition, to reside at a distance in the country ; and on returning home, was confined to her bed three weeks with typhus fever, which had been brought home by him after visiting three cases of this disease in succession. Before he was well clear of this, another, and a sorer trouble befel him. His second son, Robert, who, through his own earnest wish, long persisted in, notwithstanding every effort to induce him to abandon it, had been apprenticed to the sea, was, together with the vessel and crew to which he belonged, lost. Mr. Miller's own account of this sad event is affecting. " The last time the 'Beaufront' (for that was the name of the vessel) was in, I was on board twice and dined with the captain. He spoke of my boy in very pleasing terms, not only for his attention to his duty, in the vessel, but also his conduct generally ; that it was marked by all on board, who sometimes, on account of this, ridiculed him as a Methodist. This inspired my heart with the hope that the many prayers I had offered on his behalf were being answered. I bid my dear boy farewell, but little thought it was for the last time. It was then October, and our hope was that he would return in time again to spend his Christmas-day with us. In due time they sailed from Newcastle for London, in company with another vessel of the same firm. But a storm came on and the two ships parted. The Beaufront being a larger vessel, went out to sea, where she must have sunk with every soul on board, and amongst them my dear boy. Alas ! alas ! this is a severe trial for me—a dark and mysterious dispensation. But, O Lord, thou hast said, ' What I do thou knowest not now, but thou shalt know hereafter ;' and I would say, ' The Lord gave and the Lord taketh away, blessed be the name of the Lord.' "

He continued, with great firmness and vigor, to perform his peaceful labors amidst all his afflictions, and to be honored to snatch from ruin many of the hapless objects of his care. Emma —— was a fine sharp-looking girl, of but sixteen years of age. She had been brought up in a Sunday-school, but, alas ! had fallen a prey to temptation, and gone with those

" whose feet go down to death, whose steps take
hold of hell." She had been on the streets but fourteen days, when far from being satisfied with such a
life of drunkenness and debauchery, she had become
intensely disgusted with it, and was overwhelmed
with remorse and misery for her present conduct.
Unable to continue in it longer, and yet seeing no
way of escape, she was seriously contemplating self-
destruction. It was a solemn crisis in her history,
and Providence interposed for her rescue. By what
seemed accident she met with one of her companions
in vice and shame, to whom she opened her mind.
"Go to Mr. Miller, then, the Missionary of Broadwall," said the other unhappy creature, " if you
don't like the streets ; he'll do all he can to get you
into a penitentiary." This was just what she wanted.
Hepe dawned upon her darkened spirit. She instantly
felt assured it was the way of escape, and accordingly went to his house the same day. " Having," says
Mr. Miller, " obtained all needful information, I provided her a lodging, and then made my way to her
parents. I found them to be respectable people.
They kept a laundry, and said that the girl being
fully competent to the work, was of great service to
them. The mother agreed with me that it would
be best for her to go into an asylum, but appointed
a time when she would come to my house and see
her child. She accordingly came, and after some
preliminary conversation I sent for Emma, who was
ignorant of her mother's being there. She came

into the parlor, and the scene which then presented itself was one of the most affecting I ever witnessed. Hard indeed—a very stone, must be that heart that could have gazed upon it unmoved. We left them alone together for a short time, after which I re-entered the room, and proposed we should all kneel together in prayer, and seek the divine guidance and blessing in reference to the course that should be taken. Immediately all united in prayer. It was a solemn and touching season. In a few days she was sent, through the Southwark Female Mission, to the London Penitentiary, where she conducted herself well." She corresponded occasionally with Mr. Miller, and always expressed the most lively gratitude for his kindness in rescuing her from shame and ruin. At the end of six months she left the asylum, but continued to visit Mr. Miller, and, at last, became the wife of a respectable green-grocer.

● Allusion has been made to his deepfelt sympathy with the temporal sufferings of the poor around him, and his efforts for their relief and rescue. Every day brought occasion for the exercise of these, and called forth some fresh design. In December of this year, some saw-mills in his district caught fire, and conveyed it to the cottages of four poor families living near. A number of men, under pretence of *saving* their goods, entered their cottages, and plundered or destroyed almost the whole of them. Mr. Miller having first mentioned the matter to Lord Ashley, and obtained a handsome subscription from that nobleman, proceeded to draw up an appeal to the wealthy families around, and soon succeeded in replacing the goods of these plundered poor, and in scattering gladness again over their darkened homes and hearts.

"Poor, yet making many rich," is a Christian paradox that was strikingly exemplified in him, and the blessings of many that had been "ready to perish" came upon him. Mr. B—— was a tall and fine-looking man, of nearly seventy years of age. He was found, with his wife, by Mr. Miller, in circumstances of great temporal privation, and extreme spiritual darkness and insensibility; "without God, and having no hope in the world." Both were afterwards led, through his assiduous and persevering labors, to a saving and satisfying acquaintance with Christ, and introduced to the fellowship of Christian believers at Surrey Chapel. Mr. B—— was also provided by Mr. Miller with a truck, and furnished with a quantity of firewood, with which to enter into business; and earned for himself and aged wife a comfortable maintenance. He was subsequently taken into the service of the excellent Messrs. Harris & Co., of Broadwall, as a watchman, and acquitted himself with great satisfaction to them. He regarded Mr. Miller as his best earthly friend, and was accustomed to look to him for counsel on every occasion. "I am old enough," said he, "to be your father; but you, rather, are a father to me, and more than a father." Towards the close of the present year, 1846, Mr. B—— was visited with severe personal affliction, which increased rapidly, till it terminated in death. "I visited him," says Mr. Miller, "on the third day after the attack. He said, 'My dear friend, I know I shall not get better of this bout; you have been a kind friend to me for between five and six years, do not now leave me for a single day, for I shall not be long here, and I don't want to have anything in my ears but the word of God. Oh! what a mercy it is that I should have been permitted to hear of the way of salvation for poor sinners!' I had previously visited him, daily, but after this I did so twice each day; and when his sight was gone, he would say, as he heard my footsteps in the room, 'Is that Mr. Miller?' He was favored with great peace through believing. His favorite portion of Scripture was the eighth chapter of Romans. He died rejoicing in the Lord as his rock and his strength, and was interred at the expense of his excellent masters. Before the funeral left the house, I visited the family, addressed them on a portion of Scripture suitable to the occasion, and engaged with them in prayer. This exercise was very solemn, and productive of good to a son-in-law, whom I have since been called to visit."

In the midst of these benevolent and useful labors, he received the mournful intelligence of his mother's death. From the time he became the subject of religion, he had exerted himself to promote her spiritual welfare. With a view to this object, he had kept up a frequent correspondence with her. Although there does not appear decisive evidence of her conversion to God, yet there is some reason to hope concerning her. In a letter addressed to him by the Rev. S. Bowen, of Macclesfield, that gentleman says,—"Your good mother is not in Macclesfield at present ; as long as she tarried here, she was very punctual in her attendance upon the means, and, so far as I could see, conducted herself in every way very becomingly." On receiving the sad tidings of her death, he immediately resolved to hasten to Manchester, the place where the melancholy event had taken place, to render to her remains the last tribute of filial reverence and love. It was on Saturday, the 5th June, 1847. He gathered his family around him in domestic worship, read John xi., expatiating with much feeling on different parts of the sadly-pleasing narrative therein recorded, then for the last time knelt with them in prayer. In devotion, probably from the peculiar circumstances of the time, he was singularly copious, earnest, and solemn. How affecting to those who were present is the memory of that hour ! He then proceeded to fulfil an engagement he had made with Lord Ashley, relative to the approaching meeting of the friends of his ragged school, at which his lordship had promised to preside, and to arrange some affairs affected by his sudden call from London ; and in the evening left by the mail train for Manchester. He was not, however, permitted ever to see that town, or to advance far upon the way. As the train approached the Wolverton station, it was, through some remissness of one of the policemen, turned into a siding, which threw it into a violent collision with the carriages there stationed. Mr. Miller and six other passengers were killed upon the spot.

It is a remarkable and pleasing fact, stated by a surviving fellow-passenger, that Mr. Miller and the party accompanying him in the same carriage had agreed to close the day with devotion, and at the time when the sudden and solemn event took place, were actually engaged in singing the Evening Hymn. How appropriate to that event are the words of that hymn!

> "Teach me to live that I may dread
> My grave as little as my bed:
> Teach me to die, that so I may
> Rise glorious at the judgment-day," &c.

When searched, after death, his pockets were found filled with papers containing plans of usefulness, and printed notices of the annual meeting of his ragged school, which was to have taken place the week following. His intention was to obtain assistance for these during his absence in the country, and thus, in his case, is beautifully seen

> "The ruling passion strong in death."

"Blessed is that servant whom his Lord, when he cometh, shall find so doing!"

The report of his death went forth through the whole community almost with the rapidity and force of an electric shock. Among all classes it was felt that a real and great public loss had been sustained. This was especially the case with those who had best known his works and worth. "We have lost," exclaimed the Committee of the London City Mission, "one of our very best missionaries. He has been for seven years in the employ of the Mission; never was there a more truly missionary spirit possessed by any individual; he was constantly devising schemes of usefulness, and seemed to live for other people rather than for himself." Lord Ashley, who, with characteristic sagacity, magnanimity, and generosity, had discerned and appreciated his worth, notwithstanding his distance from him in social position, and had fought with him side by side in the great conflict against ignorance, vice, and misery, gave repeated utterance to the tenderest lamentations, reminding us of Judah's generous and noble bard, when pouring forth his sorrowful and beautiful elegies to the mountains of Gilboa, where "the shield of the mighty had been vilely cast away," and the form of his beloved Jonathan, "the beauty of Israel," had fallen a gory and ghastly corpse. Resolutions were passed and forwarded to his widow by the Committee of the Religions Tract Society and that of its auxiliary at Surrey Chapel, and by the various schools with which he was associated, expressive of their sense of his

worth, and of the greatness of the loss which they,
and the public in general, as well as his family, had
sustained.   Lord Ashley first, and afterwards the
Committee of the Mission, under the same feeling,
appealed to the Board of the North Western Rail-
way Company for compensation to his family, and
that Board, responsively to the feeling, voted a
handsome provision for his widow, and for the education of his two older children ; while the public,
in a grateful sense of his value, adopted the younger
ones, and speedily lodged them in those noble institutions, the public orphan schools of the metropolis.
Nor were the poor, degraded, and wretched people
for whom he had lived, insensible to the greatness
of the loss they had suffered.   This was affectingly
shown, especially at the funeral, which took place
on Thursday, June 10.

As his remains were conveyed to Kensall Green
Cemetery, the place selected for their reposal, a vast
concourse of people, from all parts of the neighborhood, followed them, giving the most affecting expression of their deep grief.

"Living," said the Rev. John Branch, of Waterloo Road Chapel, shortly after the event, "in the
neighborhood, I am constantly hearing the lamentations of the poor at this occurrence.   Nor is this
feeling confined to pious individuals, or to those
alone who have been benefited by his visits.   Even
the wicked and profligate seem to feel that they
have lost a friend.   On the day of his funeral, many

of the shops were partially closed in Broadwall. Small domiciles, where the poor people sell firewood, hearthstone, cats' meat, &c., had one or more shutters up, and most of the private houses had the shutters closed as a testimony of respect for their departed friend. Groups of very poor people were on that day seen at the corners of the streets lamenting their loss, some with tears. One poor Irishwoman said, in my hearing, 'God help me, what shall I do now Mr. Miller is gone! and sure he wished us well.' On a subsequent occasion this poor woman remarked to me, 'I wish I had followed his advice; I have tried very hard sometimes. Drink is my ruin. Mr. Miller was always at me about drink. I thought, at one time, he would have made a good job of me. I used to leave off for three weeks at a time, but I went back again. And now, O Lord! what shall I do? Mr. Miller is dead!' Here she wept bitterly. On my pressing upon her attention the fact, that her sin was ruinous if persisted in, and that God would help her if she sought his help, she replied, 'Ruinous! did you say? You *may* say that. Everything is in pawn again, and the children are nearly starved. I kept sober until Mr. Miller was put under the turf, after I heard he was dead. I could not do less, out of respect for him. But now *he* is gone, it is *all* gone.' On the day of the funeral, upon inquiring for the house, a man said to me, 'Do you want Mr. Miller's house, sir?—it is further on.' 'Did you know Mr.

Miller?' I inquired. 'Know him, sir? I should think I ought,' was the reply. 'He was the man who, under God, convinced me of my sin, and took me to a place of worship.' I met another person shortly afterwards, who told me that he was a teacher in the ragged school, and had been brought to a saving acquaintance with the truth through Mr. Miller's visits. Perhaps the most remarkable expression of attachment manifested by the poor, was the numbers who followed the mournful procession in its way to the cemetery at Kensall Green. Unfortunately for them, the course of the procession from Broadwall was over Waterloo Bridge, at which a toll of one halfpenny is demanded of every passenger who passes over on foot; and such was the poverty of this humble but warm-hearted funeral *cortège*, that numbers were obliged to return, when they had accompanied the remains of their religious instructor so far, not having sufficient to pay the toll. I looked at them at this spot from the coach-window,—saw their tears, and heard their lamentations.

"It would occupy too large a space to attempt to relate all I have heard at different times respecting Mr. Miller's influence on the district; but I cannot help noticing the shock that was felt at the workhouse of St. Saviour's and Christ Church Union, which he visited generally. One poor man told me, that of all the troubles he had passed through, and all the losses he had sustained—and they were very many—he had never suffered such a loss before. 'Ah!' said a poor woman in the sick ward, with whom I was reasoning concerning the extent and consequent impropriety of her grief as a follower of Christ, 'you don't know, sir, how great our loss is. If God's people lose their pastor—and that is a great loss—they can go to another; but I can scarcely leave my bed, and Mr. Miller CAME to us. How some of us have reckoned the time until he arrived! Oh, pray that I may be enabled to reckon this among the "all things that work together for good."'

"On entering a court in Broadwall, to visit a poor man one day, a short time since, there was a sad disturbance. Some of the people were quarrelling and fighting, and a group of persons were standing at the entrance of the court, to whom I observed, 'This is sad work.' 'Yes, sir,' replied one of the men, 'we want poor Mr. Miller here again. He used to quiet us.' Nor were his visits valued alone by the very poor. The poor, in general, in this part, seem to feel that they have lost a friend, who constantly had their best interests at heart, and one who was ever ready to serve them."

A large body of his missionary brethren followed him to the grave, and an impressive address was delivered by the Rev. John Robinson, one of the General Secretaries to the City Mission. On the evening of the following Sabbath, a funeral sermon was preached by his pastor, the Rev, James Sherman, at Surrey Chapel, when the doors were crowded by multitudes of the poor, who eagerly sought to hear the last of him who, in life and death, had been their faithful, their devoted friend.

The character of Mr. Miller is sufficiently evident from the foregoing pages. A few lines will compose his portrait. Though uneducated, he was in no de-gree coarse ; though unlettered, he was not scantily endowed with mental gifts. His understanding was vigorous, and distinguished for strong common sense. On all practical questions his mind was prompt and powerful in operation, and his views clear, sound, and comprehensive. He had real piety, but it dis-covered itself chiefly in action. His great charac-teristics were simple, disinterested, and generous kindness of heart, and unconquerable energy and firmness of will. There was sometimes an appear-ance of egotism, but this is only what ordinarily at-tends an earnest spirit and powerful will, and is per-haps, in some degree, inseparable from these. Tak-ing him all in all, he was a fine sample of sanctified humanity, and of missionary piety and philanthropy. And in him is verified most fully and forcibly the beautiful language of Lord Brougham · " Resting from his labors, he bequeathed his memory to the gen-cration whom his works have blessed, and sleeps under the humble but not inglorious epitaph com-memorating one in whom mankind lost a friend, and no man got rid of an enemy."

Thoughts.

In closing these brief Memoirs, a variety of important reflections are suggested : a few only shall be mentioned. The first has reference to the *condition of our metropolitan population.* We have had some painful glimpses of the state of the people among whom Mr. Miller labored ; these glimpses, however, but very faintly and imperfectly reveal to us the depth and extent of the mental, moral, and physical debasement and misery and the social disorder in which they exist. Yet it is a melancholy fact, that in this respect it is by no means worse than that of a very large proportion of the population of London ; in fact, it is far from being as bad. Without subscribing to all the inferences invidiously drawn from it by a fierce French orator, or seeing in it, as he professes to do, the dark and sure prognostic of England's approaching downfall, we must nevertheless acknowledge that the condition of a large proportion of the population of our great metropolis is in all respects most appalling. It is high time that public attention should be most earnestly directed to this state of things, and every effort put forth for its immediate and universal amelioration.

Another reflection arising out of this brief recital
has relation to the *true remedy* for their condition.
Enlightened and sound legislation, practical science,
secular education, sanitary regulations, and improved
physical circumstances generally, may accomplish
much, and should by all means be applied to the
utmost. Moral means may achieve still more. The
temperance movement, in particular, strikes at the
root of the great mass of moral and social disorders
that prevail among us, and it will be a bright omen
of approaching good to society and to men, when the
influential classes of the country shall throw themselves heart and hand into that sublime enterprise.
But these alone will not expel the great plague. It
proceeds from a cause that lies too deep for them to
reach and control. From within, "out of the heart,
proceed evil thoughts, adulteries, fornications, theft,
covetousness, murders, and such like." These are
the streams that desolate society ; the lava waves
that burn up in it all that is lovely and blest. In
nine cases out of ten, these are the causes, more or
less directly, of all outward suffering ; and there can
be no removal of the great moral, social, and physical malady till it is traced to this its true source, and is
combated by means that will grapple effectually with
it here. On the other hand, whatever avails to rec-
tify the depravity of the spirit, avails also, sooner or
later, to heal almost every other disorder. " This,
sir, is no place to serve God in," said a poor woman
residing in one of the lodging-houses of the Mint,

when brought under the power of religion ; and immediately she removed into a better locality, and sought improved outward circumstances. Such is the uniform effect of the recovery of the spirit to religion and to virtue. But this recovery no merely human means can effect. It is the peculiar work of "the glorious gospel of the blessed God." This is the divine remedy. Not only is it the power of God to salvation, to them that believe, both Jew and Greek, but also it is fitted to command belief. "Faith cometh by hearing." This the facts recorded in the above short narrative fully prove. Mr. Miller himself is a remarkable instance of rescue, from what might have seemed a hopeless depth of moral debasement and misery, and the sufficiency of the gospel as a means of spiritual renovation. And almost all the cases recorded in it are additional instances of this. Nor were it difficult to increase their number a thousand-fold. There was a woman, the wife of a gentleman of eminence—a woman who had sunk into habits of the grossest vice, and appeared to have gone beyond the possibility of recovery. For some reason she had been taken up by the police and lodged in a station-house ; while here, she extracted the steel busk from her stays, and breaking it into halves, succeeded with their ragged ends in severing some of the arteries of her body. She then leaned over the rails, in the hope she would bleed to death, but having fainted, her noise attracted the attention of the other prisoners, who hastened to her help. Medical aid was procured, and her wounds bound up. Again she meditated removing her bandages, tearing up her wounds, and renewing the fatal process of draining her body of the vital current. A missionary visited her at this juncture, and read to her from the word of God the marvellous and soul-subduing text, "God so loved the world that he gave his only-begotten Son, that whosoever believeth in him should not perish, but have everlasting life ;" and asking the policeman to kneel with him, prayed to God in her behalf. "Is it possible," thought she, "that this stranger can pray for *me*, that he has sought and found me just when, for the second time, I meditated my own destruction ?" From that time she became a perfectly new character. She returned to her home, which she has ever since adorned and blessed. She is now a member of a Christian church, and is exemplary both as a mother and a wife.

And no marvel. There is a singular, a divine adaptation in the gospel thus applied, to meet the deep-felt wants of a fallen spirit, to command its sympathies, its confidence, and its love ; to awaken its loftiest aspirations and its hopes, to quicken its palsied susceptibilities and energies, and raise it from helpless prostration to moral uprightness, majesty, and strength. It has, accordingly, ever been the glory of Christianity that it has gone down with its warm and living sympathies to the deepest abysses of human darkness, debasement, and sorrow, brought

up thence the spirits that seemed to have sunk
furthest from the sphere of help and hope, and re-
animated them, when ready to perish, with new and
immortal life—that it has rushed to the rescue of
the most helplessly enthralled, and achieved its
grandest triumphs where every other agency had
failed, and every human hope had perished.

Another thought, suggested by what has passed
before us, is the *necessity of thorough systematic
domiciliary visitation* for the dissemination of the
influences of Christianity. The great bulk of our
metropolitan population never enter a Protestant
place of worship, or come within reach of the public
ministrations of our sanctuaries. Some are so ignorant as to have no idea of the use and purpose of
these. A house was visited in Waterloo Road,
where, in one room, were assembled a great-grand-
father, a grandmother, two grandchildren, and four
great-grandchildren. Not one knew anything of
letters, nor anything of Christ, and all were so utterly ignorant of everything pertaining to religion, that
when the visitor knelt down for prayer, they all
burst into a laugh at the strangeness of his posture,
repeatedly stopped him with inquiries of the simplest
kind imaginable, and then, on his rising, wonderingly
said, " Be we all to get up ?" Another wretched
woman, who had attended an Irishman in Maryle-
bone during his last moments, and at his earnest request had sent for the clergyman of the parish, and
but a short time before he expired, had obtained for

him the administration of the Lord's Supper, said
to a missionary who called in just after his spirit
had fled, "I am afraid it was not done quite properly, for," raising the dead man's lip, "you see he
couldn't get the bread down ; do you think it is all
right ?"

And those who are better taught are in general
too far fallen to have any desire or esteem for the
public services of the sanctuary.   Vast numbers,
also, are utterly unable, from their condition and
circumstances, ever to show themselves there, however disposed, or indeed to emerge by daylight from
the dark retreats where they hide themselves with
their misery and shame.   Hundreds of females, in
the very prime of life, labor day and night, and for
seven days in the week, without being able to do
more than keep body and soul together.   For the
making of a shirt, which costs them at least a long
half-day's closest application, they receive seven or
five farthings.   At this wearying task they toil till
their forefingers are often completely ploughed up,
and the bitter tears start from their eyes ; and then,
when the task is finished, are not unfrequently sent
back without their money, because the blood from
their fingers has tinged the shirts.   Rarely have they
more garments than suffice to cover their persons,
and *hardly* do they obtain what avails to support
existence.   Often near mid-day, sitting down to the
first scanty meal of tea, without sugar, and of stale
and butterless bread ; and at the end of the day,

boiling up some weak remnant of coffee for the last. Hundreds of tailors work, with their wives, day and night to obtain an average wage of five to six shillings per week. And the case is no better with many in other departments of honorable labor. There was a man, a native of the county of Essex, who had formerly occupied a respectable position as a shoemaker at the West end of London. Through improvidence and dissipation, he had fallen in his circumstances by degrees, until at length he had settled in one of the most miserable localities as " a translator" of old boots and shoes into *new* ones. His miserable room lay about a foot beneath the surface of the ground. For a floor, he had only the bare earth, with a few broken fragments here and there. The walls on every hand were black with smoke. The only window was small ; many of the panes of glass were broken, but their places were so supplied with paper, that the objects within were hardly visible. His own appearance was in keeping with that of his room. His beard was long and dark, and his entire person almost as black as his walls with smoke and dirt. He could not, without difficulty, be recognized in his dark hole as a living being. He had no body linen of any kind, and had not worn any for more than two years. In fact, a short fustian jacket, and a pair of fustian trousers, both worn till they were as smooth and thin as a piece of brown paper, constituted the whole of his wardrobe. He had no bed, and had not lain upon one for upwards of ten years.

A wood-seated chair without a back on which he sat to work, a large tea-tray, defaced and rusted, which, resting on a massive stone, formed his stall; and another large stone, situated at the opposite side of the hearth, for the accommodation of any friends that might come to visit him, together with an old coffee-kettle and a few broken pots, formed his entire stock of household furniture. During the day he labored in his honorable and useful work of " translation," and when exhausted at night, put his head in his hand, his elbow on the hob, and slept. In these circumstances of degradation and wretchedness, he uttered no complaint, and insinuated no request to be relieved, for he regarded them as a just retribution for his neglect of former opportunities. He was fully alive to his degradation, yet never sought to proclaim it to others, or in any way to excite their sympathies. He looked upon it as the hand of God. Often he thought of public worship, but looked at himself as forever cut off from attending it. This wretched man was visited, instructed in the way of life, until it became evident that he was a changed man. He was then furnished with clothing sufficiently good to enable him to appear in the house of God. He thenceforth regularly attended thrice a-day, and has been for three years a creditable member of the church at Surrey Chapel. But for a systematic domiciliary visitation, he must, humanly speaking, have been left in darkness and lost in sin. And in this respect there are thousands, and tens of thousands, in his circumstances. By these, they are necessarily cut off from the public means of religious instruction, and must either have the gospel carried to them or perish for lack of knowledge.

Another thought, suggested by this narrative, is the *value of lay agency* in the exposition and application of the remedy. Of this, the facts here recorded are demonstrative. And they are far from standing alone. There are innumerable others equally decisive. The religious history of our own country, of America, of India, and Polynesia, are crowded with them. Let the value of this agency be reckoned by its actual usefulness in every land where it has been employed, and whether viewed among the red Indian population of the wilds of North America, or the more refined and effeminate millions that swarm on the sultry plains of Hindostan, the rude islanders of the Southern Sea, or the more civilized masses of the population of Britain, everywhere it will be found to be immense. Evils there are, undoubtedly, incidental to its use. But they are not necessary, and the only proper effect of the fact is, to call forth greater care and effort, well and wisely to direct the mighty power. Here lies the whole difficulty :—The selection of the right men—men of real, simple, earnest piety and kindness—of sound understanding and practical character, of activity, energy, and perseverance, and their judicious and effective direction. And surely, if it is thus valuable, it ought, especially in these eventful and solemn times, to be most diligently and extensively applied. If an effective breakwater is to be thrown up against the advancing tide of Popery and superstition, and the thick darkness that already covers the degraded millions of our city population is to be rolled away, every agency must be invoked and laboriously plied. "Blessed are ye that sow beside all waters, *and send forth thither the feet of the ox and of the ass.*"

We gather, finally, from the facts that have passed before us, *how much may be done by individuals of the humblest rank and least favorable circumstances,* through earnest philanthropy, holy zeal, and consecrated energy. These were the great characteristics of Mr. Miller, and these, humanly speaking, the only sources of his success in the benevolent and pious labors in which he was engaged. And wherever these are found, similar results are found in connection with them. Witness the life of Thomas Cranfield, "the useful Christian," of Sarah Martin, and a thousand others. There is, in fact, no calculating the extent of good which any individual may effect if but his heart be fully set upon it, and there be thrown into it all his might. Were every Christian thus to act, what—oh, what might be hoped to be achieved! The salvation of God would then break forth like the light of morning.

The darkness, superstition, vice, and disorders of many generations would melt away as mist, and the age come quickly on when earth, in all her dwellings, would enjoy a continual Sabbath, and celebrate responsively to heaven a world-wide and a lasting jubilee.

THE END,

VALUABLE BOOKS

PUBLISHED BY

ROBERT CARTER & BROTHERS

285 BROADWAY, NEW YORK.

---

* *Those having on asterisk prefixed to them are new Books, or new Edition, which have not been on former lists.*

---

*Abeel's (Rev. David) Life. By his Nephew, 18mo.	$	50
Abercrombie's Contest and The Armour. 32mo. gilt		25
Adam's Three Divine Sisters—Faith, Hope, &c.		60
Advice to a Young Christian. By a Village Pastor. With an Introduction by Rev. Dr. Alexander. 18mo.		30
Alleine's Gospel Promises. 18mo.		30
—————— Life and Letters. 12mo.		60
Alexander's Counsels to the Young. 32mo. gilt		25
Ancient History of the Egyptians, Assyrians, Chaldeans, Medes, Lydians, Carthaginians, Persians, Macedonians, &c. 4 vols. 12mo. cloth or sheep		2 00
*Anderson—The Annals of the English Bible, by Christopher Anderson. Revised, abridged, and continued by Rev. Samuel Irenæus Prime. 8vo.		
—————— The Family Book; or, The Genius and Design of the Domestic Constitution. 12mo.		75
Australia, the Loss of the Brig, by Fire. 18mo.		25
'Bagster—The Genuineness, Authenticity, and Inspiration of the Sacred Volume. 12mo.		60

Baxter's Saint's Rest. Large type. 12mc   60
——— Call to the Unconverted. 18mo.   30
——— Choice Works. 12mo.   60
Bible Expositor. 18mo.   50
Bickersteth's Treatise on Prayer. 18mo.   40
——— Treatise on the Lord's Supper. 18mo   30
Blunt's Undesigned Coincidences in the Writings both
  of the Old and New Testaments, an Argument of
  their Veracity. 8vo.   1 25
Bogatzky's Golden Treasury, 18mo.   50
Bonar's Night of Weeping. 18mo.   30
——— Story of Grace. 18mo.   30
Bonnet's Family of Bethany. 18mo.   40
——— Meditations on the Lord's Prayer. 18mo.   40
Borrow's Bible and Gypsies of Spain. 8vo. cloth   75
Boston's Four-fold State. 18mo.   50
——— Crook in the Lot. 18mo.   30
Brown's Explication of the Asssembly's Catechism. 12mo. 60
Bridges on the Christian Ministry. 8vo.   1 50
——— On the Proverbs. 8vo.   2 00
*——— On the cxix Psalm. New edition. 8vo.   1 00
*——— Memoir of Mary Jane Graham. 8vo   1 00
*——— Works. 3 vols. 8vo. containing the above   5 00
*Brown's Concordance. New and neat ed. 24mo.   20
          Do.   *gilt edge.*   30
Buchanan's Comfort in Affliction. 18mo.   40
*——— On the Holy Spirit. 18mo. 2d edition   50
Bunbury's Glory, Glory, Glory, and other Narratives.
  18mo.   25
Butler's Complete Works. 8vo,   1 50
——— Sermons, alone. 8vo.   1 00
——— Analogy, alone. 8vo.   75
——— and Wilson's Analogy. 8vc.   1 25
'Bunyan's Pilgrim's Progress, fine edition, large type,
  with eight illustrations by Howland. 12mo.   1 00
          Do.   do.   *extra gilt*   1 50
          Do.   do.   clcose type, 18mo.   50
          Jerusalem Sinner Saved. 18mo.   50

Bunyan's Greatness of the Soul. 18mo.   50
Burn's Christian Fragments. 18mo.   40

Calvin on Secret Providence. 18mo.   25
Cameron's Farmer's Daughter. 18mo.   30
Catechisms—The Assembly's Catechism. Per hundred   1 25
        Do. with Proofs   3 00
———— Brown's Short Catechism. Per hundred   1 25
———— Smyth's Ecclesiastical Catechism. 18mo.   25
———— Willison's Communicant's. 18mo.   10
———— Key to the Assembly's Catechism. 18mo.   20
*Cecil's Works; comprising his Original Thoughts on
      Scripture, Sermons, Miscellanies, and Re
      mains. 3 vols. 12mo. with portrait   3 00
———— Remains. Separate   60
———— Original Thoughts on Scripture. Separate   1 00
Charnock's Choice Works. 12mo.   60
*Chalmers' Sermons, enlarged by the addition of his
      Posthumous Sermons. 2 vols. 8vo. With a
      fine portrait   3 00
———— Lectures on Romans. 8vo.   1 50
———— Miscellanies. 8vo.   1 50
———— Select Works; comprising the above. 4 vols.
      8vo. *With portrait.*   6 00
———— Evidences of Christian Revelation. 2 vols.   1 25
———— Natural Theology. 2 vols.   1 25
———— Moral Philosophy   60
———— Commercial Discourses   60
———— Astronomical Discourses   60
Christian Retirement. 12mo.   75
———— Experience. By the same Author. 18mo.   50
Clark's Walk about Zion. 12mo.   75
———— Pastor's Testimony   75
———— Awake, Thou Sleeper   75
———— Young Disciple   88
———— Gathered Fragments   1 00
Clarke's Daily Scripture Promises. 32mo. gilt   30
Colquhoun's World's Religion. 18mo.   30

*Cowper—The Works of William Cowper; comprising his Life, Letters, and Poems, now first collected by the introduction of Cowper's Private Correspondence. Edited by the Rev. T. S. Grimshaw. With numerous illustrations on steel, and a fine portrait by Ritchie, 1 vol. royal 8vo.   3 00

———— Do.   do.   sheep   3 50

———— Do.   do   half-mor.   4 00

———— Do.   do.   cloth extra gilt   4 00

———— Do.   do.   mor. extra   5 00

Cunningham's World without Souls. 18mo.   30

Cumming's Message from God. 18mo.   30

———— Christ Receiving Sinners   30

Davies' Sermons. 3 vols. 12mo.   2 00

*Davidson's Connexions. New edit. 8vo.   1 50

David's Psalms, in metre. Large type. 12mo. embossed   75

———— Do.   do.   gilt edge   1 00

———— Do.   do.   Turkey mor.   2 00

———— Do. 18mo. good type   plain sheep   38

———— Do.   "   "   "   Turkey mor.   1 25

———— Do. 48mo. very neat pocket edition,   mor.   25

———— Do.   "   "   "   gilt edge   31

———— Do.   "   "   "   tucks   50

D'Aubigne's History of the Reformation. *Carefully revised*, with various additions not hitherto published. 4 vols. 12mo.   half cloth   1 50

———— Do.   "   "   full cloth   1 75

———— Do.   "   "   4th vol. half-cloth   38

———— Do.   full cloth   50

———— Do.   "   '   Complete in 1 vol.   1 00

———— Life of Cromwell. 12mo.   50

———— Germany, England, and Scotland. 12mo.   75

———— Luther and Calvin. 18mo.   25

Dick's Lectures on Acts. 8vo.   50

*Dickinson's Scenes from Sacred History. 2d ed. 12mo.   1 00

Doddridge's Rise and Progress. 18mo.   40
—— Life of Colonel Gardiner. 18mo.   30
Duncan's Sacred Philosophy of the Seasons. 4 vols   3 00
—— Life. By his Son. With portrait. 12mo.   75
—— Tales of the Scottish Peasantry. 18mo.   50
—— Cottage Fireside. 18mo.   40
—— (Mrs.) Life of Mary Lundie Duncan. 18mo.   50
—— —— Life of George A. Lundie. 18mo.   50
—— —— Memoir of George B. Phillips. 18mo.   25

*Erskine's Gospel Sonnets. New and beautiful edition. 1 00
*English Pulpit, a collection of Sermons by the most
' eminent English Divines of England. 8vo.

*Farr's History of the Egyptians, 12mo.
*—— History of the Persians, 12mo.
*—— History of the Assyrians, Chaldeans, Medes, Ly-
        dians, and Carthaginians, 12mo.
—— History of the Macedonians, the Selucidæ in
        Syria, and Parthians. 12mo.
Ferguson's Roman Republic. 8vo.   1 50
Fisk's Memorial of the Holy Land. With steel plates   1 00
Fleury's Life of David. 12mo.   60
Foster's Essays, on Decision of Character, &c., large
        type, fine edition. 12mo.   75
—— close type. 18mo.   50
Ford's Decapolis. 18mo,   25
Free Church Pulpit; consisting of Discourses by the
        most eminent Divines of the Free Church of Scot-
        land. 3 vols. 8vo.   5 00
Fry (Caroline) The Listener. 2 vols. in one   1 00
—— Christ our Law. 12mo.   60
—— Sabbath Musings. 18mo.   40
—— The Scripture Reader's Guide. 18mo.   30

Geological Cosmogony. By a Layman. 18mo.   30
God in the Storm. 18mo.   25

Grabam's (Mrs. Isabella) Life and Writings   12mc.   60
—— (Miss Mary J.) Life and Works.   8vo.   1 00
—— Test of Truth.   Separate.   18mo.   50
*Green—The Life of the Rev. Ashabel Green, D.D., by
the Rev. Dr. Jones, of Philadelphia.   8vo.
Griffith's Live while you Live.   18mo.   30

Haldane's Exposition of Romans.   8vo.   2 50
Hamilton's Life in Earnest—Mount of Olives—Harp on
the Willows—Thankfulness—and Life of Bishop
Hall, each   30
*Hamilton—The Happy Home.   With 12 illustrations
by Howland.   18mo.   50
Hawker's Poor Man's Morning Portion.   12mo.   60
——   "   Evening Portion.   "   60
—— Zion's Pilgrim.   18mo.   30
Hervey's Meditations   "   40
Hetherington's History of the Church of Scotland   1 50
Henry's (Matth.) Method for Prayer   40
—— Communicant's Companion.   18mo.   40
—— Daily Communion with God.   "   30
—— Pleasantness of a Religious Life.   "   30
—— Choice Works.   12mo.   60
*Henry, Philip, Life of.   18mo.   50
Hill's (George) Lectures on Divinity.   8vo.   2 00
—— (Rowland) Life.   By Sidney.   12mo.   75
*History of the Puritans in England, and the Pilgrim
Fathers, by the Rev. W. H. Stowell and D. Wilson,
F.S.A., with two steel plates.   12mo.   1 00
History of the Reformation in Europe.   18mo.   40
Housman's Life and Remains.   12mo.   75
Horne's Introduction.   2 vols. royal 8vo. half cloth   3 50
—— Do.   do.   1 vol. sheep   4 00
—— Do.   do.   2 vols. cloth   4 00
—— Do.   do.   2 vols. library style   5 00
—— Bishop, Commentary on the Book of Psalms   1 50
Howel's Life—Perfect Peace.   18mo.   30

Howe's Redeemer's Tears and other Essays. 18mo. 50
Huss (Jno.) Life. Translated from the German 25

Jacobus on Matthew. With a Harmony. Illustrated. 75
—— Questions on do. 18mo. 15
—— On Mark, Luke, and John (preparing.)
James' Anxious Inquirer. 18mo. 30
—— True Christian. " 30
—— Widow Directed. 18mo. 30
Janeway's Heaven upon Earth. 12mo. 60
—— Token for Children. 18mo. 30
Jay's Morning Exercises. 12mo. 75
—— Evening " " 75
—— Christian Contemplated. 18mo. 40
—— Jubilee Memorial. " 30
Jerram's Tribute to a beloved and only Daughter. 30

Key to the Shorter Catechism. 18mo. 20
Kennedy's (Grace) Profession is not Principle. 18mo. 30
—— Jessy Allan, the Lame Girl. 18mo. 25
Krummacher's Martyr Lamb. 18mo. 40
———— Elijah the Tishbite, " 40
———— Last Days of Elisha. . 12mo. 75

Life in New York. 18mo. 40
Lowrie's Letters to Sabbath School Children. 18mo. 25
Lockwood's Memoir. By his Father. 18mo. 40
Luther's Commentary on Galatians. 8vo. 1 50

Mackay—The Wyckliffites; or, England in the 15th
        Century. 75
Martin's (Sarah) Life. 18mo. 30
Martyn's (Henry) Life. 12mo. 60
Mason's Essays on the Church. 12mo. 60
—— " on Episcopacy. " 60
Martyrs and Covenanters of Scotland. 18mo. 40
Malcom on the Atonement. 18mo. 30

McCrindell—The Convent, a Narrative. 18mo.   **50**
McGilvray's Peace in Believing. 18mo.   25
McLeod's Life and Power of True Godliness. 12mo.   60
McCheyne's (Rev. Robert Murray) Works. 2 vols. 8vo.   00
——— Life, Lectures, and Letters. Separate.   50
——— Sermons. Separate.   2 00
——— Familiar Letters from the Holy Land. 18mo.   50
*McFarlane—The Mountains of the Bible, their Scenes
    and their Lessons, with four illustrations on steel. 12mo. 75
——— Do.   Do.   extra gilt   1 25
Meikle's Solitude Sweetened. 12mo.   60
Miller's (Rev. Dr. Samuel) Memoir of Rev. Dr. Nisbet.   75
——— (Rev. John) Design of the Church. 12mo.   60
Michael Kemp, the Farmer's Lad. 18mo.   40
Moffat's Southern Africa. 12mo.   **75**
Monod's Lucilla; or, the Reading of the Bible. 18mo.   40
*More (Hannah)—The Book of Private Devotion.
              Large type, elegant edition, 18mo.   50
——— Do.   do   do   extra gilt   75
——— Do.   do.   small edition, 32mo.   20
——— Do.   do.   "   gilt   30
Missions, the Origin and History of. By Choules and
    Smith. With 25 steel plates. 4to.   3 50
Morell's Historical and Critical View of the Specula-
    tive Philosophy of Europe in the 19th Century   3 00
My School Boy Days. 18mo.   30
My Youthful Companions. 18mo.   30
    The above two bound in 1 vol.   50

Newton's (Rev. John) Works. 2 vols. 8vo.   3 00
——— Life. Separate. 18mo.   30
Noel's Infant Piety. 18mo.   25
North American Indians. Illustrated. 18mo.   50

Olmsted's Thoughts and Counsels for the Impenitent   50
Old White Meeting-House. 18mo.   **40**
*Opie On Lying. New edition, 18mo.

Owen on Spiritual Mindedness. 12mo.   60
Old Humphrey's Observations; Addresses; Thoughts
   for the Thoughtful; Homely Hints; Walks in London; Country Strolls; Old Sea Captain; Grandpa-
   rents; Isle of Wight; Pithy Papers; and Pleasant
   Tales, 11 vols. Each   40

Paley's Horæ Paulinæ. 12mo.   75
Paterson on the Assembly's Shorter Catechism. 18mo.   50
Pike's True Happiness. 18mo.   30
—— Religion and Eternal Life. 18mo.   30
—— Divine Origin of Christianity. 18mo.   30
Philip's Devotional Guides. 2 vols. 12mo.   1 50
—— Marys.   40
—— Marthas.   40
—— Lydias.   40
—— Hannahs.   40
—— Love of the Spirit.   40
—— Young Man's Closet Library.
Pollok's Course of Time, the most elegant edition ever
   published; printed on superfine paper. 16mo. with
   portrait. Cloth.   1 00
—— —— gilt, cloth, extra,   1 50
—— —— Turkey morocco, gilt   2 00
—— —— small copy, close type. 18mo.   40
— Life, Letters, and Remains. By the Rev. James
     Scott, D.D. With portrait. 16mo.   1 00
—— Do. gilt cloth, extra   1 50
—— Tales of the Scottish Covenanters, printed on
     large paper, uniform with the above. With
     portrait   75
—— Do.   do.   small copy. 18mo.   50
—— Helen of the Glen. 18mo.   25
—— Persecuted Family. 18mo.   25
—— Ralph Gemmell. 18mo.   25
Portens' Lectures on Matthew 12mo.   60

Retrospect (The) by Aliquis. 18mo.	40
*Richmond's Domestic Portraiture, edited by Bicker-	
steth. New and elegant edition. 12mo.	75
—— Annals of the Poor. 18mo.	40
Rogers' Jacob's Well. 18mo.	40
Romaine on Faith. 12mo.	60
—— Letters. 12mo.	6C
Rutherford's Letters, new edition,—preparing.	
Scott's Force of Truth. 18mo.	25
Scougal's Works. 18mo.	40
Select Works of James. Venn, Wilson, Philip, and Jay.	
Eight complete works in 1 volume. Royal 8vo.	1 50
Select Christian Authors; comprising Doddridge, Wil-	
berforce, Adams, Halyburton, à Kempis, &c. With	
Introductory Essays by Dr. Chalmers, Bishop Wil-	
son, and others. 2 vols. 8vo.	2 00
Serle's Christian Remembrancer. 18mo.	50
Sinner's Friend. 18mo.	25
*Sigourney (Mrs. L. H.) Water Drops. 18mo. 2d edit.	50
*—— The Girl's Book, 18mo With illustrations.	
—— The Boy's Book, "	
*Sinclair's Modern Accomplishments	75
*—— Modern Society	75
—— Charlie Seymour. 18mo.	30
Simeon's Life, by Carus ; with Introductory Essay by	
Bishop McIlvaine. With portrait. 8vo.	2 00
Sir Roland Ashton. By Lady Catharine Long	75
Sketches of Sermons on the Parables and Miracles of	
Christ by the Author of the Pulpit Cyclopædia. 12mo.	75
Smyth's Bereaved Parents Consoled. 12mo.	75
Sorrowing Yet Rejoicing. 18mo.	30
Do. 32mo. gilt	30
*Spring (Rev. Gardiner, D.D.)—A Pastor's Tribute to	
one of his Flock, or Memoirs of the late Hannah L.	
Murray. With portrait. 8vo.	
Stevenson's Christ on the Cross. 12mo.	75

Stevenson's Lord our Shepherd. 12mo.	60
Sumner's Exposition of Matthew and Mark. 12mo.	75
Suddard's British Pulpit. 2 vols. 8vo.	3 00
Symington on the Atonement. 12mo.	75
—— on the Dominion. 12mo.	75

Tacitus' Works translated. Edited by Murphy. 8vo.	2 00
Tennent's Life. 18mo.	25
Tholuck's Circle of Human Life. 18mo.	30
Taylor's (Jane) Life and Correspondence. 18mo.	40
—— Contributions of Q. Q. 2 vols.	80
—— Original Poems. 18mo.	30
—— Display, a Tale. 18mo.	30
—— Mother and Daughter	30
—— Essays in Rhyme. 18mo.	30
—— Original Poems and Poetical Remains. With 12 fine illustrations by Howland. 18mo.	
—— (Isaac) Loyola; or, Jesuitism in its Rudiments.	1 00
—— Natural History of Enthusiasm. 12mo.	75
—— (Jeremy) Sermons, complete in one vol. 8vo.	? 00
Turretine's Complete Works, in the original Latin	
The Theological Sketch Book, or Skeletons of Sermons, so arranged as to constitute a complete body of Divinity. From Simeon, Hannam, Benson, &c. 2 vols.	3 00
Tyng's Lectures on the Law and Gospel. New edition, large type, with a fine portrait. 8vo.	1 50
—— Christ is All. 8vo. With portrait.	1 50
—— Israel of God. 8vo. enlarged edition.	1 50
—— Recollections of England. 12mo.	1 00
Thucydides' History of the Peloponnesian War. Translated by William Smith. 8vo.	1 25
Turnbull's Genius of Scotland, or Sketches of Scottish Scenery, Literature, and Religion. 12mo.	1 00
—— Pulpit Orators of France and Switzerland, with Sketches of their Character and Specimens of their Eloquence. With portrait of Fenelon.	1 50

Waterbury's Book for the Sabbath. 18mo.   40
Whately's Kingdom of Christ and Errors of Romanism.   75
Whitecross' Anecdotes on the Assembly's Catechism   30
White's (Hugh) Meditation on Prayer. 18mo.   40
—— Believer; a Series of Discourses. 18mo.   40
—— Practical Reflections on the Second Advent. 18mo. 40
—— (Henry Kirke) Complete Works. With Life by
        Southey. 8vo.
—— Do.   extra gilt
Wilson's Lights and Shadows of Scottish Life. 18mo.   50
*—— Do. on large paper, 16mo., with eight illustra-
        tions, from original drawings, by Croome,
        Billings, &c. engraved by Howland.   75
—— Do.   do.   extra gilt   1 25
Winslow on Personal Declension and Revival   60
Wylie's Journey over the Region of Fulfilled Prophecy.   30

Xenophon's Whole Works. Translated.   2 00

*Young's Night Thoughts. Elegant edition, 16mo.
        with portrait   1 00
—— Do;   do   extra gilt   1 50

BOOK IS DUE ON
STAMPED BELOW

NITIAL FINE OF 25 C
ASSESSED FOR FAILURE TO
ON THE DATE DUE.
TO 50 CENTS O
ON THE

Lightning Source UK Ltd.
Milton Keynes UK
UKOW06f0945010216

267515UK00018B/660/P